COIN COLLECTING

FOR BEGINNERS 2024

The New Up-To-Date Guide to Easily Start Your World Coin
Collection and Learn How to Identify, Value, Preserve
and Profit from Your Hobby

LINCOLN FORD

TABLE OF CONTENTS

INTRODUCTION

Welcome to *Coin Collecting for Beginners 2024;* I am thrilled to be your guide on this exciting journey into the captivating world of coin collecting. As a passionate numismatist with a deep appreciation for the history, artistry, and cultural significance of coins, I have dedicated years to perfecting the craft of coin collecting. Now, I am eager to share my knowledge and expertise with you.

Coins have been an integral part of human civilization for centuries, serving as a means of trade, a reflection of cultural identity, and a glimpse into the past. They are more than mere pieces of metal; they are artifacts that connect us to different eras, civilizations, and stories. By collecting coins, we have the opportunity to immerse ourselves in a hobby that combines art, history, and the thrill of discovery.

In this comprehensive guide, we will embark on a journey that covers every aspect of coin collecting. We will begin by exploring the fascinating world of numismatics and understanding its history and significance. We will delve into the basics of coin collecting, examining different types of coins, coin series, and themes. With practical advice, we will learn how to start our own coin collections and identify coins with investment potential.

Before we dive into the exciting world of coin collecting, we will prepare ourselves for the journey ahead. We will set goals for our collections, establish budgets, build a solid knowledge base, and create efficient storage systems to preserve our coins for future generations.

As we progress through the chapters, we will explore different collecting methods and approaches. Whether you choose to build a comprehensive collection, focus on specific themes or time periods, or specialize in a single country or region, there is a collecting style that suits your interests and aspirations.

We will also delve into the joys and benefits of coin collecting, discovering how it enhances our appreciation for art, connects us with the past, and provides endless opportunities for research and learning. We will uncover the various sources where we can locate coins, from coin shops and dealers to online marketplaces, auctions, and even metal-detecting adventures.

Equipped with essential tools and knowledge, we will learn how to preserve and protect our coin collections, ensuring their longevity and integrity. From proper handling and cleaning techniques to choosing the right storage options, we will safeguard our valuable treasures. We will also explore the intricacies of coin grading, understanding the importance of evaluating the condition and quality of our coins to determine their value.

In this book, we will not only focus on traditional coin collecting but also explore specialized areas of numismatics. We will uncover the allure of commemorative and special edition coins, delve into the world of bullion coins as an investment opportunity, and take a closer look at the unique and limited-edition issues that make coin collecting even more fascinating.

Moreover, we will explore the global landscape of coins, dedicating a chapter to the exploration of the world coin series. From popular coin series from around the world to the cultural and historical significance of coins from different countries and regions, we will appreciate the diverse and captivating nature of coins across borders.

But coin collecting is not limited to adults alone. In a special chapter, we will engage young numismatists in the hobby, introducing coin collecting to children in a fun and educational way. Through activities and tips, we will nurture their interest and cultivate a lifelong passion for coins.

As we near the end of our journey, we will uncover strategies for selling our coin collections, ensuring we maximize our returns. We will also equip ourselves with the knowledge to avoid counterfeits and scams, protecting our collections and investments. Finally, we will discuss the perfect timing to sell coins, understanding market cycles and trends to optimize profitability.

In *Coin Collecting for Beginners 2024*, I have aimed to provide a comprehensive guide that simplifies complex concepts, offers practical guidance, and inspires readers to embark on their own coin collecting journeys. With a deep appreciation for the beauty, history, and cultural significance of coins, I hope to ignite your passion for this rewarding hobby and empower you to create a collection that reflects your unique interests and aspirations.

So, let us embark on this thrilling adventure together as we uncover the secrets and treasures that await us in the world of coin collecting. May this book be your trusted companion and resource as you embark on a lifelong journey of exploration, discovery, and connection through the fascinating realm of numismatics.

CHAPTER 1

WHAT IS NUMISMATICS

T he study of coins and money, as well as coin-like objects, is known as numismatics. The value of coins as historical evidence was recognized even in antiquity, but the systematic development of coin study as a separate discipline with its own methodology began only in the late eighteenth century with the work of Joseph Hilarius Eckhel, an Austrian priest whose Doctrina Numorum

Veterum (Vienna, 1793–1799) was an eight-volume attempt to comprehend all of ancient Greek and Roman coinage. Eckhel's work inspired few immediate imitators, but it served as a catalyst for the methodical cataloging and analysis of Europe's largest numismatic collections. Chairs in numismatics were created in the big universities in Austria, and the important cabinets were put under the control of professional historians and archaeologists. Interest in coinage may be related to the maturity of the nation and its roots in North America, where there is no academic tradition (but, most importantly, no actual discovery of old coins). The main cities (Boston, New York, Philadelphia, Montreal, and Chicago) saw the emergence of "numismatic and antiquarian" organizations in the late 1850s and early 1860s. Some of them drew the attention of notable academics, but the field never made it into the university system. Numismatics is seldom taught in the United States, and when it is, it is primarily as a supplement to other interests. Given the present attitude of schools and institutions toward their numismatic holdings, it is difficult to see when the study will play more than a minimal role, even in graduate programs.

- Numismatics is the study of coins and other forms of currency, and it is commonly associated with the appraisal and collection of rare coins.
- Numismatists study the physical properties, manufacturing technology, and historical context of currency specimens.
- Rare and collectible coins may trade for significantly more than their nominal face value or commodity melt value, and they are frequently removed from circulation and viewed as investments rather than actual money.

- Numerous clubs, societies, and other organizations have been formed to promote numismatic studies.
- In the United States, becoming a numismatist requires completing specialized classes and passing a 200-question test.

UNDERSTANDING THE ROLE OF NUMISMATICS

Numismatics is distinct from monetary history and economics. Numismatists investigate the physical characteristics of payment media rather than their use and function in an economy. Although the terms numismatics and coin collecting are frequently used interchangeably, numismatics denotes a more in-depth study than simply collecting coins. Although all numismatists are coin collectors, not all coin collectors are numismatists. It is widely assumed that numismatics emerged during the early European Renaissance as part of a quest to rediscover all things classical.

The term "numismatics" was first used in English in 1829, derived from the adjective numismatic, which translates to "of coins," and was obtained from the French word numismatique, which was derived from the Latin word numismatist.

Numismatists are experts who research the physical technology and historical background of coins and money. Coins or other tokens that are rare or unique or have a special history that can be documented are thought to be the most interesting to study and valuable as collectibles. Specimens that exhibit flaws in the manufacturing process of striking the coins or printing the notes are especially noteworthy.

Currency Value

Rare units of currency can trade for far more than their face value or the commodity value of their physical substance due to their properties and value as collectibles. Some twentieth-century US silver quarters, for example, with a face value of 25 cents and a silver melt value of a few dollars, can trade for tens of thousands of dollars.

Collectors remove them from circulation to use as collections or investments rather than using them at face value. This is analogous to the operation of "Gresham's Law," which states that under legal tender laws, bad (less valuable) money drives good (more valuable) money out of the market. Gresham's Law is applied to an even greater extent in the case of rare and collectible coins or other monetary tokens; the coins are not only withdrawn from circulation but also cease to be money in an economic sense.

Numismatic Organizations

Numerous organizations exist to promote the study, research, and progress of the numismatic sciences. The American Numismatic Society, for example, was founded in New York City in 1858 to foster public appreciation of coins, medals, and currencies and has since cultivated more than 800,000 objects dating back to 650 BCE, as well as a numismatic library with 100,000 books and artifacts. Among the other numismatic organizations are:

- Guild of Ancient Coin Collectors
- America's Archaeological Institute

- The Canadian Numismatic Association is a monetary organization in Canada.
- Czech Numismatic Society (Czech Numismatic Society)
- International Numismatic Commission/International Numismatic Commission
- Israel's Numismatic Society
- Asian Numismatic Society
- The Professional Numismatists Guild is an organization of professional numismatists.
- The Royal Numismatic Society is a numismatic organization.
- The Australian Numismatic Association
- New Zealand's Royal Numismatic Society

NUMISMATIC HISTORY

The study and analysis of how people use money, as well as the collection of various types of money, coins, and other forms of consideration, is referred to as numismatics. Numismatics has a centuries-long history. Coin collecting, on the other hand, most likely began with the invention of currency.

Prior to the nineteenth century, coin collecting was mostly an individual activity cherished by the nobility, religious elite, and kings. During the Roman Empire, rulers such as Caesar Augustus gathered coins from different locations to use as bargaining chips in trade talks and to give as gifts to visitors.

There was a coin collecting explosion during the Renaissance era, with Europeans fascinated by the materials and collections of previous civilizations. The coins with engraved images of animals, mythical gods and goddesses, and rulers were particularly appealing. Francesco Petrarca, or Petrarch, was an Italian scholar and poet who is regarded as the first Renaissance coin collector and the catalyst for the 14th-century numismatic boom.

Numismatics grew in popularity over time. Coin collecting societies sprang up all over the world in the 1800s, including the New York-based American Numismatics Society.

Coin collecting has grown in popularity since the advent of the Internet, attracting a larger audience of enthusiasts. Potential and experienced numismatists have unlimited access to information, tools, and numismatic communities.

Fields of Study

Because there are so many different kinds of cash, coins, and notes, the study of numismatics has been divided into many subfields. Each subfield specializes in a particular type of numismatic collectible. Notaphily, exonumia, and scripophily are three of the most prevalent.

The study and collecting of paper money is known as notaphily. Notaphily is derived from the Latin word "nota," which means "paper money," and the Greek word philia, which means "love." Notaphilists are people who collect paper money, such as banknotes.

The study and collecting of coins, including tokens, medals, and other similar things, is known as exonumia. Exonumia is a combination of the Greek words exo, which means "out of," and nummus, which means "coin." These items can be used as currency or to commemorate events and accomplishments. Exonumia is primarily concerned with commemorative military medals awarded for service in war and military expeditions.

The study of securities, such as stocks and bond certificates, is known as scripophily. Scripophily is a combination of the Greek word for love and the English word "scrip" for ownership. Scripophilists often collect these instruments because they are beautiful, rare, and historically significant. Because the issue of stock certificates is mostly an archaic procedure, this pastime is far more difficult to pursue than the others.

HOW TO BECOME A NUMISMATIST

A numismatist, also known as a coin grader, is a professional who collects, analyzes, and grades collectible coins, currency, and other similar items. Prospective numismatists in the United States must join the American Numismatic Association (ANA), complete required courses, and pass an exam.

The numismatist program is made up of six courses, each of which focuses on a different topic. After finishing the courses, the candidate must pass a 200-question exam. Once the requirements are met, the candidate is awarded a diploma confirming their expertise in the field of numismatics.

Additional training may be required to cement knowledge and skills. Additional tools and resources are available from the ANA and other professional organizations.

Numismatic Fun Facts

- In 1252, Florence, Italy, became the first city in the world to mint its own gold coins.
- Although collecting old coins is a worldwide pastime, it was once considered a royal pastime enjoyed only by kings and queens.
- The United States Secret Service was founded in 1865 to combat counterfeit money at a time when one-third of all federally issued paper money was thought to be counterfeit. Following the murder of President William McKinley in 1902, the Secret Service was tasked with safeguarding the president for the first time.

CHAPTER 2

BASICS OF COIN COLLECTING

C oin collecting has been around since the 12th century and is still a popular hobby for people of all ages all over the world. There are numerous reasons for beginning a coin collection, which is commonly referred to as 'numismatics' by enthusiasts.

Saving specific £1, £2, or 50p coins found in pocket change is one of the cheapest ways to start collecting. After all, they will never lose their value and can be spent if you become bored with the hobby.

Some collectors get a rush from holding a beautiful piece of craftwork in their palm, where they can fully appreciate its age, weight, and history.

For others, coin collecting is a way of life rather than a hobby. Rare artifacts are prized for their beauty and scarcity and are sometimes sought-after using metal detectors.

Whatever your reason for being interested in numismatics, this introduction to coin collecting will teach you a few basic rules so you can build a collection you'll be proud of.

THE BASIC PARTS OF A COIN

Before beginning a collection, it's important to understand the fundamentals, such as the different areas of a coin.

- The head: Also known as the 'obverse,' this side typically features an image of a bust or portrait as well as the year it was minted.
- The tail, also known as the 'reverse,' displays the coin's face value.
- The rim is a raised area that surrounds the diameter of the obverse and reverse sides.
- The relief: The portion of a coin's design that protrudes above the surface.
- The edge, also known as the 'third side,' is often grooved but can also be ornamental or plain.

- The legend is the lettering or inscription that identifies the country of issue as well as the face value of the coin. It may bear the designer's initials.
- The field: Any flat surface with no inscriptions that serves as the coin's background.

THE DIFFERENT COIN TYPES

When you first start collecting coins, you may not be aware of all the different types of coins available.

Here are some of the most common types you'll encounter:

- Error coins: Any coin that has a flaw that sets it apart from other similar examples. These are frequently extremely rare, difficult to obtain, and expensive.
- Proof coins: These coins are specially minted for collectors and are highly valued for their distinctive visual appeal. They have a flawless design and finish that is of the highest quality. Coin collecting's pinnacle.
- Brilliant Uncirculated coins: Coins have never been in circulation but have a fine mint appearance and luster. A proof coin has a slightly lower definition.
- Commemorative coins: Issued to commemorate a special event or to pay tribute to a notable person, Commemorative Coins can often be valuable in their own right.
- Bullion coins are coins made of precious metals like gold, platinum, and silver.

- Ancient coins: Outstanding pieces of history, often handcrafted, dating back to Roman or Greek times.
- Circulating coins, also known as business strikes, are coins that are widely used on a daily basis.
- Worldwide coins: Any coin from a country other than the United Kingdom.

TIPS FOR PURCHASING COINS ONLINE

First and foremost, investigate the seller's reputation. This should go without saying, but enthusiastic purchasers are still being taken advantage of by a few individuals who are willing to dump their cleaned and damaged rubbish on the unknowing, despite being called up on it several times by previous customers. Most auction platforms allow you to rate sellers and examine other purchasers' ratings.

Second, review and comprehend the seller's return policy. What can be done if the coin in your hand does not resemble the coin in the photos on the internet? Will you be refunded in full? Who is responsible for shipping costs?

Third, carefully examine the coin photos. Photos should be taken in a straight line, not at an angle. Some dealers conceal hairlines (evidence of cleaning) and other flaws by photographing the item at an acute angle, causing the light to reflect differently and the hairlines to disappear. You may ask the vendor for a new picture, or you could just go on to the next coin.

Fourth, many rare, or "key," coins are being counterfeited in large quantities, primarily in China. It's an issue as ancient as money itself, and counterfeits abound on internet auction sites. Inexperienced numismatists may get enthusiastic about the inexpensive 1916-D mercury dime and believe they've won an auction, only to send it off for grading and have it returned as a fake. As a result, when purchasing key coins, only purchase ones that have been certified and encapsulated by a credible third-party grader.

Finally, beware of internet coin vendors who claim to know nothing about the item or coinage in general or who pretend to be settling an estate. As a general rule, these people do know something about coins and use their ignorance to create a layer of plausible deniability in the event that their problem coins are discovered.

While most people reading this have probably heard this advice before, it never hurts to go over it again. Each season, legendary football coach Vince Lombardi would introduce himself to that year's team of professionals by holding up a football and saying, "Gentlemen, this is a football." Many were undoubtedly surprised, if not outraged that he would say something so basic to a group of professionals. Lombardi, on the other hand, believed that each season should begin with the fundamentals of the game. Instill superiority in terms of the fundamentals. He believed that his team could never achieve greatness unless they mastered the fundamentals. Similarly, numismatists should master these fundamentals and review them on a regular basis.

HOW TO START A COIN COLLECTION

With so many different coins to choose from, starting a collection can be intimidating at first.

Learn everything you can about coins before spending money on them. Begin with the loose change in your pocket and get acquainted with its pieces, inscriptions, pictures, the material it is made of, and the sort of coin it is.

After you've mastered the fundamentals, you'll be able to weigh your options for compiling your collection.

Collectors typically specialize in one of four major categories:

Theme

The most frequent approach to begin started with numismatics is to collect by subject - the choices are unlimited. Simply choose a subject that has been portrayed on a coin, and you're ready to start. It might be a fictional character, a famous person, animals, automobiles, trains, flowers, structures, landmarks, sports, or sporting events. Unsurprisingly, the Olympic Games are the most popular coin collecting topic in the world, closely followed by football and military history.

Historical Significance

Coins from a given era are popular among historical lovers. You may be interested in a certain time period (for example, WW2 from 1939 to 1945) or a specific year, such as England's World Cup victory in 1966. Perhaps you could collect every coin minted from one year, such as the

Crown through the Farthing, before doing the same for another. Another intriguing technique to collect by year is to gather coins with distinct mint markings.

Type or Denomination

If you collect coins depending on their monetary worth, you have the option of getting every significant design ever displayed, such as those on a Penny or Farthing. You could also collect all of the year types or different mint marks.

Origin Country

If you want to learn about a country's culture and history, collecting coins is a great way to do so. Although British coins are obviously popular, those issued in Canada and America also provide valuable insight into their Presidents and historical periods, such as the Gold Rush, Civil War, and Wild West era.

WHAT IS YOUR MOTIVATION FOR COLLECTING?

When embarking on this fantastic journey, it's critical to understand why you've been inspired to do so.

Here are a few of the most common reasons we've heard:

- Interest was passed down from generation to generation.
- Interested in specific topics (queens, wars, sports, movies, etc.)
- Take use of the visual references that coins provide.
- By chance, I discovered an interesting coin.
- Save foreign coins from international travel.

- Coins should be admired for their aesthetic worth.
- As an example, consider following the Royal Mint's work.
- Collect for the value of their bullion.
- Consider it a long-term investment.

Although there is no correct or incorrect way to begin a coin collection, discovering the secret may help mold your views and collecting habits in the long run.

The golden rule of coin collecting, in our opinion, is to only collect coins that you like or find interesting. If you follow this rule, you'll never get tired of your new hobby.

How to Store Coins

Coins are made of metal, but they are easily damaged, so they must be handled and stored carefully.

When you first start off, your coins are likely to be of lower worth, and the simplest place to keep them is in a coin tray (shown below) or cabinet.

When you start collecting more valuable coins, you'll need a better storage solution.

Single coin envelopes made of acid-free paper are ideal for storing coins. To avoid oxidation or scratches, special airtight envelopes or albums may be used to keep or exhibit a collection of individual coins.

How to Clean Coins

There is a proper technique to clean coins, and doing it incorrectly may typically lower their worth.

We do not recommend cleaning a coin unless absolutely necessary.

If you really want to clean a coin, hire a numismatic expert to do it for you. On the other hand, never use chemicals or abrasive cleaning tools on coins.

Collect, Learn, and Have Fun

This enthralling hobby can quickly get a hold of you, whether you want to collect for pleasure or treasure.

When they first start collecting, few collectors know what kinds of coins they want to collect. Most people start by purchasing a variety of denominations or types until they find a specific area of interest.

As with any hobby or specialty, novice collectors are more likely to make mistakes than more experienced collectors. However, this is not something that beginners should be concerned about.

However, before purchasing any coin, you should think long and hard about it. Is it the style you like and within your pricing range? If you respond 'no' to any of these questions, it's most likely not the appropriate one for you.

Depending on your budget, it's always a good idea to buy the highest quality coin you can afford at the time. Adopting this attitude will pay off in the long run. After all, it's usually preferable to own a few valuable coins that pique your interest rather than a larger collection that fails to pique your interest.

Remember that coin collecting should be a fun hobby. Take your time, do your research, and learn about the various coins available. It could take months or years to build a collection - and coin knowledge - that you're proud to show off.

| CHAPTER 3 |

WHAT IS WORTH COLLECTING?

oin collecting has been practiced for millennia. Coins were the primary currency when people used the barter system to exchange goods and trade. However, as time passed, the monetary system changed, boosting the value of coinage. There are several varieties of precious coins available to collectors all around the world.

Many coin collectors do so because they are fascinated by the history and stories behind the coins. Collectors are interested in preserving the history of coins that tell a story about a specific time or event. Other coin collectors may be interested in the coin's value and how much it is worth. Coin collecting may be a pastime for some and a source of income for others.

The rarest coins in history are generally the most valuable. The more valuable a coin, the more rare it is. Coins made of gold or silver or in good condition are also more useful. Collectors prefer coins that are in mint or uncirculated condition. Coin collecting became popular many years ago and has only grown in popularity since then.

People are becoming increasingly interested in coin collecting, and the hobby is growing in popularity.

6 MOST VALUABLE COINS OF ALL TIME

Saint-Gaudens Double Eagle

Because of its history and scarcity, the Saint-Gaudens Double Eagle is a valuable coin for collectors. The coin was created by Augustus Saint-Gaudens. Furthermore, it was coined from 1907 until 1933. There were 445,500 Saint-Gaudens Double Eagles minted in total, with only a few dozen known to exist today. The gold coin is regarded as one of the most incredible coins ever created. Collectors prize the Saint-Gaudens Double Eagle for its rarity and historical significance.

Flowing Hair Silver Dollar

Because it is the first silver dollar coin minted by the United States Mint, the Flowing Hair Silver Dollar is valuable to coin collectors. Only 1,758 coins were produced when the coin was minted in 1794. The Flowing Hair Silver Dollar is also valuable due to its scarcity. The currency has only six known surviving examples.

Brasher Doubloon

Because it is a rare and early American gold coin, the Brasher Doubloon is valuable to coin collectors. Ephraim Brasher minted the Brasher Doubloon in 1787. In New York City, he worked as a goldsmith and silversmith. Brasher's initials, "EB," are imprinted on the coin's breast. There are only seven Brasher Doubloons known to exist, and each one is unique in design. The Brasher Doubloon is the first gold coin ever minted in the United States, as well as the most valuable and rare eighteenth-century gold coin.

Edward III. Florin

Due to its scarcity and unique history, the Edward III florin was a valuable coin for collectors. The coin was only struck for a short time during the reign of King Edward III of England before being withdrawn. As a consequence, very few of these coins survive today, making them very desirable among collectors. Furthermore, the coin has a one-of-a-kind design that is not found in any other English currency, making it even more desirable.

Umayyad Gold Dinar

For collectors, the Umayyad Gold Dinar is valued for various reasons. First and foremost, it is a lovely coin with intricate designs that are both eye-catching and one-of-a-kind. Second, it is a rare currency since it was only struck for a short time during the Umayyad era. Collectors see it as precious and sought-after cash as a result. Finally, the Gold Dinar has a lengthy and deep history, which makes it a thrilling and coveted currency.

Canadian Gold Maple Leaf

Collectors prize the Canadian Gold Maple Leaf coin owing to its beautiful design and 0.9999 gold purity. The coin was first minted in 1979, and the Royal Canadian Mint has produced it annually since then. Each coin contains one troy ounce of gold and is worth CAD 50. The Gold Maple Leaf is regarded as one of the most amazing coins in the world, and its popularity has only risen in recent years.

RARE AND VALUABLE COINS

Many people are curious about the monetary value of rare coins. There are definitely numerous precious coins in circulation.

However, distinguishing a rare coin from a common coin is not always simple. Some of the most valuable items seem to have few, if any, distinguishing features that would make them stand out to a novice collector.

Here is a list of some of the most precious and uncommon coins. We'll explain why some rare coins are valuable and why others aren't.

The following is a list of rare coins that are more likely to be found in circulation (pocket change) or in heirloom collections. The majority of the list is made up of "D" and "S" coins from the Denver Mint and the San Francisco Mint, respectively.

Several are 20th-century error coins, and roughly half of these US coins contain precious metals. Interestingly, several different types of small cents, such as Indian Head pennies and Wheat pennies, appear on the list.

In its first year of production (1909), the Lincoln cent included the designer's initials, Victor D. Brenner. The lettering was removed after only one year due to an odd controversy. It is still considered one of the most classic collectible coins in US history.

1914-D Lincoln Wheat Cent:

The 1914-D penny had one of the series' lowest mintages. The Denver Mint struck only 1,193,000 coins that year.

1955 Lincoln Cent Doubled Die Obverse (DDO)

Die doubling is a common form of mistake that may occur at the mint. The 1955 Lincoln penny is likely the most famous example of this kind of inaccuracy in US currency history.

1969-S Lincoln Cent Doubled Die

The doubled die error was also present in a small portion of the 1969-S penny mintage from San Francisco.

1972 Lincoln Cent Doubled Die Obverse (DDO)

Die doubling was an issue with some of the 1972 Lincoln pennies struck in Philadelphia.

1937 Buffalo Nickel 3-Legged

A "missing leg" on Buffalo nickels produced in 1937 and 1938 was caused by an over-polished die. The 3-legged Buffalo nickel, along with the 1955 DDO penny, is one of the most notable American coin mistakes.

1916-D Mercury Dime

The Winged Liberty Head dime was originally produced in 1916. The design was instantly dubbed the "Mercury Dime" because of its similarity to the Roman god of battle. With approximately 264,000 coins struck, 1916-D has by far the lowest mintage in the series.

1901-S Barber Quarter:

The Barber coinage of the late nineteenth and early twentieth centuries was unpopular at the time it was issued. However, in the century that followed, these coins became considerably more uncommon and valuable.

1916 Standing Liberty Quarter

The Standing Liberty quarter is one of the most collectible old coins ever produced by the United States Mint. The year this design debuted was 1916. Partway through the 1917 mintage, the design was changed amid controversy so that Lady Liberty's exposed breast was covered with chain mail.

1932-D, Washington Quarter

George Washington appeared on the quarter for the first time in 1932. Denver's entire mintage was just 436,800 coins. The new design was meant to be a one-year commemorative coin, but it has remained on the quarter coin ever since!

1932-S Washington Quarter

In 1932, the San Francisco Mint, like its Denver counterpart, produced a very small number of Washington quarters. Only 408,000 were produced.

Walking Liberty Half Dollar, 1938-D

The Walking Liberty half-dollar is still regarded as one of the most beautiful designs ever to grace a United States coin. The image is still used today for the American Silver Eagle bullion coin.

1921 Peace Dollar:

The popular Peace Dollar was introduced in 1921. The coins from the 1921 mintage all had a High Relief design. Although lovely, this creative design was cumbersome for daily usage, so the relief was reduced.

Pre-1933 U.S. Gold Coins:

Prior to 1933, gold coins were legal tender in the United States. They are 90% pure gold and come in denominations of $1, $2.50, $3, $5, $10, and $20. Collectors and gold speculators are both interested in these antique gold coins.

FACTORS AFFECTING COIN VALUE

If you are a coin collector, you are probably aware of the coin market's complexity. Obviously, each coin is minted with a specific face value, but when it comes to collectibles, the value multiplies exponentially. In fact, if the coin meets the right criteria, collectors may be willing to pay several times the face value.

Whether you collect rare coins as a hobby or as a long-term investment, you must be aware of the factors that influence the value of collectible coins in order to avoid being duped. Here are the criteria you should be aware of:

High Demand

Anything that is scarce is in high demand, and collectible coins are no exception. Collectible coins, like any other commodity, have a direct relationship between demand and price. Increased demand from the general public and the numismatic community will almost certainly result in a rise in the coin's value. This is common with old coins because they are difficult to obtain, and everyone wants them. When coin dealers run marketing campaigns to popularize their offerings, demand rises.

Mintage

Supply, like demand, is an important factor that influences the value of collectible coins at any given time. Obviously, anything that is widely available commands a lower price than something rare. The total market supply of any type of coin is determined by its initial mintage. More often than not, a coin dies at the end of the year because it is no longer minted.

As a result, its supply is set at a specific moment in time, influencing its price.

The Intrinsic Value of the Metal

Some coins are valuable and expensive simply because of their intrinsic metal value. Obviously, a coin with a high content of gold or silver will command a higher price than one with a lower content of precious metal. For example, junk silver coins such as US half-dollars, quarters, and dimes minted prior to 1965 contain 90% silver. Because of their high silver content, they are worth more than their face value. As a result, they are a good long-term investment as collectibles because they can be melted down for their high silver content.

Surviving Population

Coins that have become excessively worn and damaged are removed from circulation, implying that their surviving population is limited at any given time. The lower a coin's surviving population, the rarer it gets and the greater its value. You may look at these very rare coins, which are unlikely to be found on the market. There is no way to obtain them anywhere except for a few people and coin collectors who may have kept them. All because they are so uncommon, with a population that can be counted on the fingers!

Grade and Condition

When determining the worth of any collectible coin, you must consider its grade and condition. Grading, in essence, establishes the condition of a coin, and its grade defines its worth. A coin with a flawless mint grade is worth much more than an identical coin with just a minor defect.

The coin's grade is determined by its attractiveness, color, brilliance, strike, and preservation. Third-party grading organizations are often used to assess the grade of coins in an impartial way. When purchasing a coin as a collectible, make sure it is certified and that the grade is correct.

Unique History

A coin's unique history is an unusual factor that determines its value. A coin that would otherwise be worthless becomes a rare and valuable collectible because it has historical importance, such as being linked to a famous king or a significant historical event. The coin does not have to be ancient to be valuable historically; rather, it must be one of a kind!

Buying coins at the right price will be easier now that you understand the key criteria that determine their value. Aside from paying special attention to these factors, be sure to purchase only from a reputable dealer or collector. Whether you are a novice or an experienced collector, be certain that you choose things that deserve to be valued rather than paying for ones that are useless.

IDENTIFYING COINS WITH INVESTMENT POTENTIAL

Rare coins have historically provided significant profit potential above and beyond the underlying metal value of a coin. According to Finest Known, a rare-coin newsletter, prices of elite coins increased by more than 1,000% from 1976 to 1980 and 600% from 1982 to 1989.

Investing in rare coins is not a substitute for traditional investments in order to achieve your financial objectives. This asset, on the other hand, can help you diversify your portfolio and reduce risk.

The rare coin market has evolved dramatically over the last few decades. In the 1980s, third-party grading services were allowed to grade coins, verifying their authenticity and defining standards, removing some of the risks of investment. Furthermore, the internet provided the opportunity to gain more knowledge about coin collecting, rare coins, and coin purchasing.

If you're just getting started with rare coin investing, consider finding a mentor who can help you research the value and potential future value of coins. You can also learn about this field by attending coin shows, reading books and articles, conversing with coin dealers, and joining coin clubs.

CHAPTER 4

PREPARING FOR YOUR COIN COLLECTING JOURNEY

Coin collecting has been practiced for a long time. Everything started when people began collecting rare coins in ancient times. These coins were originally given as costly gifts, and precious metal coins were utilized as a kind of currency. Today, however, many people enjoy discovering rare coins in order to learn more about their history and to benefit from them.

People may gather coins for enjoyment. So, if you're considering taking up this activity, know that you're not alone. If you search online, you will undoubtedly come across many organizations of coin collectors from all around the globe. You may choose to join a collectors' community, particularly if you're just starting off. The best group for you is determined by why you want to collect coins. Is it to earn money, or is it simply a pastime? If the latter is the case, communities will most likely be a useful networking tool for you. However, if it is the former, you may discover novel ways to make money from your hobby.

Having said that, here's a comprehensive journey to coin collecting. It will lay out everything you need to know as you begin this fascinating journey of coin collecting. It will also teach you what kind of coins to look for, how to find them, and other useful information.

While coin collecting is enjoyable, it is not as simple as you might think. You must be deliberate about it, especially if you want to become an expert coin collector. As a result, it is important to explain why you want to start a collection. If you don't have the proper motivation to begin this hobby, there will be plenty of opportunities to make excuses. As a result, here are a few compelling reasons to begin a coin collection:

HISTORICAL SIGNIFICANCE OF COINS

Not everyone will be charmed by the thought of holding a reasonably old coin. Some, however, will. Of fact, the historical significance of ancient coins varies. Remember that the majority of these coins have a backstory that can help you determine their worth. Knowing the history of each coin will help you appreciate it more and may even encourage you to start collecting coins.

For Investment

A coin's value may often much surpass its face value. Remember that the rarer a coin is, the more valuable it is. Furthermore, certain coins, like antique artworks, gain value through time. So, if you want to make more money, sell your coins at a later time.

Rare coins may sell for tens of thousands of dollars or more. But it all boils down to selecting the right coin and working with a trustworthy dealer like Infinity Coins. As a result, if you want to make money from coin collecting, you must first conduct extensive research.

For Fun

This category includes the vast majority of people. If you enjoy finding and storing coins, coin collecting could be a great hobby for you. If you engage in this interest, you will make numerous unusual discoveries and learn a lot along the way. Curiosity can help you if you want to become an avid coin collector. Furthermore, if you enjoy doing something, it is unlikely that you will take it for granted. So, starting coin collecting for the sake of fun and adventure is a great reason.

It's an Inexpensive Hobby

A coin collection does not require a large sum of money to begin. A coin collector does not require any special tools or kits. However, if you want to earn money, you must be ready to put in the work. This might include obtaining adequate coin storage or designating an area in your house to keep the coins secure and protected from corrosion.

HOW TO GET STARTED?

It can be difficult to decide where to begin your coin collecting journey. But with determination and guidance, it is possible. Here are some pointers to get you started:

Define Your Interests

To begin, you must define your interests. Knowing them will assist you in selecting the best route. You don't want to become a random coin collector since creating a coin collection should be meaningful and personal to you.

The narrative behind a coin collection is what distinguishes it. You're meant to be the one who wrote it. However, the first step is to determine what aspects of this interest appeal to you. Simply ask yourself what piques your interest and go from there.

Choose The Coins You're Interested In

You must now decide which types of coins you want to collect, as there are several to choose from. For example, if you are interested in ancient Greece, you should collect coins from that time period. Keep in mind that you may need to do some research to find these coins.

Conduct Research

Reading up on coin collecting materials is vital in the beginning. As previously stated, coin collecting has been around for a long time. As a result, there are numerous things you should learn before you begin. Look for coin collecting books and magazines to learn more about the ins and outs of this hobby. Furthermore, educating yourself is an excellent way to avoid falling victim to dubious scams.

Join Relevant Groups and Communities

It would be beneficial if you thought about joining a coin collecting club or an online group. Join a club if you're fortunate enough to have one in your area! Joining an online community, on the other hand, works just as well. Coin collecting is a popular hobby all over the world, and if you're lucky enough to be a member of a club, you'll be able to learn all about it much faster.

It also enables you to network with others who share your interests. Furthermore, there will most likely be a facility where members can buy and sell coins, which means that joining a club will give you access to a variety of coins.

Watch Online Exhibitions

You should also look into coin collecting exhibitions and shows. These shows are now being broadcast online, so you can participate in some of them. You'd be surprised how much you can learn from others who share your interests. If you're wondering where you can get the links to some of these antique and coin collecting exhibitions, ask the members of the clubs and groups you belong to.

Invest in Proper Storage

As previously stated, you may want to find a place to keep your coins. You should put them in a place you or others may see them. However, how you store them is entirely up to you. Just make sure they're safe and secure. When it comes to delicate coins, safety is everything.

COINS YOU CAN COLLECT

Before you begin your coin collecting adventure, you should be aware of the various types of coins available. Here's a quick rundown of a handful of them:

Commemorative Coins

These are coins that are inextricably related to certain historical events. These coins were designed to commemorate significant events, as the name implies. They may also be used to commemorate the birth of a notable historical figure or the death of a prominent individual.

Proof Coins

These coins are often made for exceptional events. They are also typically produced in limited quantities and have distinguishing characteristics that make them valuable.

Bullion Coins

These coins were made from precious metals, including gold, silver, and platinum. As a result, these coins are very valued and expensive. Bullion coins are an excellent investment for those who want to start collecting coins as a way to make money.

Error Coins

These are simply incorrectly manufactured coins. It may seem strange to want to collect these, but some error coins have interesting stories behind them. As a result, they're worth a look.

Ancient Coins

These are the antique coins. It's understandable that they're difficult to find because they come from the ancient world and countries like Greece and Rome. These coins depict the likenesses of historical figures such as Julius Caesar.

East Asian Coins

Many collectors are interested in the histories of Asian countries such as Mongolia, China, Japan, and Korea. These coins are collected by a large number of coin collectors.

Latin American Coins

Latin America has a fascinating past. Many coins have been created in their ancient territories throughout the centuries. If you're interested in Latin American history or have Latin ancestors, this could be a good option for you.

WHERE AND HOW TO FIND COINS?

Metal Detecting

If you're feeling daring, you may use metal detectors to look for old coins. This isn't the most practical way to find coins. However, looking for them in historical locations may be beneficial. Before you begin your search, review the site's local rules and restrictions. You'll also need extra patience since this will need a lot of Googling. Nonetheless, if you come upon a coin, bear in mind that it is unlikely to be in excellent condition. The worse the condition, the older it is.

Flea Markets

You might also try your luck at yard sales or flea markets. These could be great places to find some rare coins. The only disadvantage of this method is determining the authenticity of the coins. But make no mistake: some of these locations may hold some genuine jewels. You simply must exercise caution.

Antique stores

If you're just starting out, these places could be a great place to start. Furthermore, some of them have online websites that provide numerous catalogs and information that may assist you in deciding which one to buy. Before purchasing anything, just ensure that the websites are genuine.

Online Dealers

Another simple approach to finding coins for your collection is via online dealers. There are several merchants to pick from on various internet and e-commerce platforms. However, you must again confirm the legitimacy of some of these online dealers. To prevent getting duped, always deal with recognized merchants.

HOW COINS ARE VALUED?

The Sheldon Scale is a tool used by coin valuers to determine the value of a coin. This scale ranges from 1 to 70, with 1 being the lowest and 70 being the highest. A coin with significant wear and tear may be assigned a P-1 Poor rating. A coin with an MS-70 Mint State Perfect grade, on the other hand, is in superb condition. As a consequence, the better the rating, the more money you may get for your currency.

Several coin and antique dealers use this scale to value their coins. However, other factors such as a coin's metal type, condition, distinctive characteristics, and mint year all influence its final cost or worth. Furthermore, these values should be used with caution since they may give themselves incorrect prices. These values, however, may be more reliable if performed by a reputable store.

Because of the Sheldon Scale, it is critical to keep your coins in good condition during your coin collecting journey. As long as you keep them up, you should be able to get good ratings and good returns.

CREATING A STORAGE SYSTEM

"Delicate" may not be the first word that comes to mind when you think of coins. But you'd be surprised how easily these small pieces of precious metal can be damaged and devalued.

Handle each coin separately. You don't want them to come into touch with each other and scratch or injure each other.

Handle your coins by the edges, not the faces.

Before handling your coins, wash your hands. Dirt and oils from your hands can tarnish the surface of the coin.

Avoid handling your coins on a hard or bare surface. When removing your coins from their case, proceed with caution. Handle them on a towel or other soft surface to prevent harm if you drop them accidentally.

You should not clean your coins. Cleaning and polishing your coins will devalue them, as strange as it may seem. Improper technique and aggressive chemicals might cause the surface to be stripped or scratched. It is preferable for your coins to be colored to represent their age.

Coin collecting is an excellent hobby that anyone can enjoy. It is not necessary to have a specific skill set or intellect to participate. You just need to be passionate about it. However, it is important to note that different people will begin collecting coins for various reasons. Whatever your purpose, coin collecting may be an interesting and educational activity.

Starting may be difficult. However, being active in groups or communities may enhance your experience. It's always preferable to share your experience with individuals who are just as interested, if not more so, as you are. Prioritize lifelong learning as well. You must continually remain up to date on coin collecting news and trends. Furthermore, you must be prepared to conduct research and stay up to date on the various forums in which you participate.

CHAPTER 5

COLLECTING METHODS AND APPROACHES

Coin collecting is an enjoyable, risk-free, and gratifying way to learn about history and the world around you. Though distinguishing cheap, ordinary cash from rare, uncirculated money might be challenging, there are techniques to make the procedure simpler and less hazardous. Knowing where to hunt for nice coins, what to look for in a purchase, and how to keep your coins secure can make it easier to start a collection.

BUILDING YOUR COLLECTION

Find A Type of Coin to Collect

There are hundreds of various coin designs available, with differences in size, denomination, origin, age, and rarity. Though it may seem difficult at first, focusing your search on a certain kind of coin can keep you focused and make the quest lot more pleasant. Remember, there is no right or wrong way to collect, so choose a coin that calls to you. Among the suggestions are:

- A cent for each year you've lived.

- One of every coin issued in the United States since World War II.

- From the year you were born, one of each country's lowest-valued coins.

Find A Good Price Range for You

Coins that are old, uncommon, misprinted, or uncirculated are cool, but they are also quite costly. Cheaper alternatives include commonly circulating coins, which may be obtained by sifting through pocket change and bank rolls or recently issued special currencies, such as the US State Quarters series.

Many foreign coins are far less expensive than their US equivalents. Look for 5-cent pieces from the Netherlands (1913-40), Canada (1922-36), and France (1898-1921) for budget collecting, as well as coins from minor nations like Luxembourg.

Look For Coins with Little Wear

Keep an eye out for flat, non-dented coins with minimal scuffs and scratches while shopping for collectibles. Look for coins that have preserved the majority of their reflecting characteristics, indicating that they have not been traded often. Collectors can expect a coin to be in reasonable shape even if it is 500 years old.

Look For Coins That Have Been Verified by Outside Sources

Whenever feasible, buy coins that have been graded for quality and authenticity by organizations such as the American Numismatic Association. Make sure specialized coins come with a certificate of authenticity from the original mint.

Feel Free to Swap

When you have a few coins in your collection, you may start trading them with other collectors. You may either trade coins online at sites like Numista or with a local coin collector near you.

When you trade coins online, you will almost always send and receive the coins by mail.

COIN PURCHASING

Visit A Coin Store in Your Area

Despite the fact that coin collecting is a rather rare pastime, many cities have at least one coin store nearby. These shops sell a large variety of coins at reasonable prices, making them ideal for beginning collectors. Most store owners are collectors at heart and can assist you in determining the worth of specific coins, connecting with other vendors, and locating excellent, up-to-date collecting materials.

- Some coin businesses will buy coins directly from customers, while others will only buy from reputable vendors.

- Dealers will often charge up to 20% more than independent sellers.

Attend Coin Auctions and Expos

Coin auctions, expos, and other events, albeit intermittent and not necessarily nearby, are terrific locations to find new coins. Auction websites such as AuctionZip can help you identify forthcoming auctions, and the American Numismatic Association maintains a list of upcoming coin and money expos on its website.

While eBay and other big markets may provide outstanding results, it is practically hard to examine or confirm the quality of a coin before purchasing. Try niche sites like Great Collections or Heritage Auctions instead.

Participate in a Coin Club

In the near term, numismatic organizations are an excellent opportunity to meet other collectors, hear about forthcoming events, and get advise on how to broaden your knowledge and collection. Long-term club members who intend to sell their coins sometimes prioritize and offer cheaper prices to friends acquired via the organization.

Online directories provided by organizations such as the American Numismatic Association may link you with local and regional groups.

Purchase from a National Mint

You may acquire specialty and commemorative coins directly from the national mint in several nations. Even if mints price more than face value, they often include a certificate of authenticity and a quality guarantee. Uncirculated and proof coins, which are significantly more valuable than their used counterparts, are also available from mints.

CALCULATING MARKET VALUE

Purchase The Book Before The Coin

This is a classic numismatic expression that says you should understand a coin before investing in it. Before making any purchases, consult current price guides, such as the printed Handbook of United States Coins or the web-based Professional Coin Grading Service. These will help you to discover and compare the current market value of various coins and grades.

For foreign coins, see country-specific guides and databases such as Numista.

Consult specialized works on ancient coins, such as Ancient Coin collecting.

Avoid buying cheap coins from skilled vendors. If an offer seems to be too good to be true, it most often is. Check to be sure a coin is genuine and hasn't been buffed or polished to mask flaws. If you discovered it at a garage sale, flea market, or similar place, the vendor might not be aware of the true worth of their goods, but specialist sellers and collectors are well aware of it.

Discover How Coins Are Graded

Coins are evaluated differently depending on the nation and appraiser, but the Official A.N.A. Grading System for United States Coins is an excellent place to start. Coins are graded on a scale of 0 to 70, with uncirculated coins receiving bonus points. Quality is denoted by letters, such as MS for Mint State or VG for Very Good. The highest grade coin in this system is designated as MS-70.

In general, appraisers in the United States are more forgiving than those in the United Kingdom, so keep in mind that a flawless coin in one country may be judged faulty in another.

Some individuals over-grade their own coins in order to make them more marketable. To prevent being duped, double-check all coins using an approved "by the book" standard.

Remember that grading is subjective, especially when done by a professional service, and that grading criteria vary over time.

Purchase a Magnifying Glass

Purchase both a low-powered and a high-powered magnifying lens for avid collectors. This will enable you to examine for minor flaws and evidence of counterfeit, such as coins with improper typefaces or crooked aesthetic features. Pay great attention to gleaming coins since features may have been polished away to make them look glossier.

Purchase a Scale

For collectors making large purchases, a portable electronic scale is a crucial investment. Weighing a coin and comparing it to collection guidelines might assist you in detecting counterfeits made of inferior materials. Weighing a coin may also help you determine its melt value or how much it would be worth if melted down into its basic ingredients.

KEEPING AND SHOWING YOUR COLLECTION

Purchase a water and fireproof safe that may be fixed to the ground for dedicated collectors. This can safeguard your investment from floods, fires, and criminals, which is particularly crucial when dealing with high-value things. If you collect extremely rare or valuable coins, consider upgrading to a safe-deposit box at your local post office or bank for further protection.

If you have home insurance that covers your coins, maintain an up-to-date inventory with photos to confirm quality.

Coins, like many other treasures, should be stored in a dry, comfortable atmosphere with low moisture. Avoid attic or basement rooms, as well as regions exposed to direct or indirect sunlight and humidity, since these may all harm your coins.

Purchase Coin Flips for Single Coins

Coin flips are typically 2x2 holders made of vinyl or cardboard. They are similar to record or trading card sleeves in that they protect your coin while enabling you to exhibit it. Poly vinyl (PVC) holders should be avoided since they may harm the coin over time, even etching the coin surface.

Purchase coin folders, boards, and albums to complete your collection. Coin album sleeves, like flips, have distinct sections that are tied together on binder-sized pages. They may be ordered with or without a binder. Coin folders and boards are specialized cardboard containers with holes for coins to be pushed into. These are often offered by kind, with separate folders for quarters, pence, and so forth.

SPECIALIZING IN A SINGLE COUNTRY OR REGION

Coin collecting is a universe unto itself, with limitless options in how one collects. While the choices might be overwhelming, making it difficult to know where to begin, there are a few basic techniques to collect pennies without being overwhelmed.

Coins with Slabbed Surfaces

Some coin collectors prefer to look for coins that have already been graded and verified. Slabbed coins are obtained from third-party grading firms and are kept in a sealed container to ensure the longevity of the collector coin.

Mint Mark and Date

Date and mint markings, which are popular among American collectors, indicate the Mint facility the piece was produced and the year it was made. The reason it is an American favorite is due in major part to the fact that each Mint often creates a set amount of coins, and when that quantity is low, discovering one of the coins becomes even more exciting!

Region

Another popular method of collecting within the numismatic community is to examine the location from whence the coin originated. Collecting coins from a certain region, whether in the United States, Europe, Asia, Canada, China, South Africa, or Australia, lets collectors carve out their niche and offers a focus on their interest.

Though these are only a few suggestions to get a beginner coin collector started, remember to select the sort of collecting that is suited for you. Slabbed coins, American coins, European coins, and so on. It is vital to go along the path that not only makes sense for your budget but also what you are interested in as a collector.

CHAPTER 6

WHY COLLECT COINS? EXPLORING THE JOYS AND BENEFITS OF COIN COLLECTING

People collect antique coins for a variety of reasons. Some individuals respect the historical worth of coins, while others love collecting various sorts of coins. Whatever your motivation, there are various advantages to collecting antique coins.

PROFITABLE

People usually collect ancient coins since they know they may earn a lot of money from them. To be certain that your currency is successful, you should constantly do research and consult with professionals. Always learn all you can about the coins you collect since it will help you make a lot more money.

Some are worth millions of dollars, and only a few individuals in the world possess them. You may join them if you continue to make wise investments in your coin collection.

It's really a terrific investment that can earn you a lot of money if you do it correctly. So, start collecting old coins now and watch how much your investment grows over time!

HISTORICAL IMPORTANCE

The excitement of discovery is one of the greatest pleasures of coin collecting. Coins are more than simply bits of metal; they are historical objects that chronicle the narrative of a country. Every coin has a tale to tell, from ancient coins with exquisite patterns to current coinage commemorating key events. Each coin is a physical piece of history, and collecting them helps individuals to learn about the many cultures and civilizations that have shaped the world. "Holding a coin enables you to understand how human civilization has evolved over time and provides insight into the thousands of lives that have gone before you."

Every antique coin has a fascinating historical backstory. Some of them date back centuries and are important to the country's history and culture.

Collecting antique coins is more than just a nice pastime or an investment in something valuable. It's also about holding a genuine piece of history in your hands; it's like holding a piece of an entire tale connected to that coin.

Having an antique Spanish coin, for example, may teach you a lot about the culture and history of Spain at that time period. The same holds true for any other country's currency.

This is what makes antique coins so intriguing and unique: their ability to take you back in time, offering you a glimpse of the world as it was centuries ago. And this is definitely a worthwhile bonus!

EDUCATIONAL POSSIBILITY

Coin collecting is a lifelong learning experience. "The more you research and study different coins, the more you learn about different eras, rulers, and past civilizations." This may be an excellent educational experience for both young and elderly collectors since it promotes lifelong learning and creates respect for many cultures and customs.

For example, you may learn about a country's or region's history by examining its coinage. You may also learn about many areas of coin manufacturing and design. Furthermore, becoming a collector allows you to understand more about economics and numismatics (the study of money). Overall, antique coins may be a terrific teaching tool for anybody interested in global history and money.

Here are some lessons that can be learned from antique coins:

- A certain country's or region's history
- Various elements of coin manufacturing and design
- Economics and numismatics (money studies)
- How to Recognize Fake Coins
- How it got to this point
- The benefit propositions
- Rarity
- It has an interesting backstory.

CULTURAL UNDERSTANDING

Coins are valued not just for their monetary value but also for their aesthetic and cultural significance. Many coins have stunning patterns and detailed features that highlight the creative abilities of the historical period in which they were made.

Financial Investment

Coin collecting, apart from the historical and aesthetic features, may also be a wise investment. While coin collecting is largely a recreational activity, it may also be a wise financial investment. "In fact, many rare coins have appreciated in value over time, making them a lucrative investment if you know what to look for and are willing to do your research." However, coin collecting should not be considered a get-rich-quick scheme, and before making any investment choices, considerable thought should be given to aspects such as market trends, conditions, and authenticity.

DIVERSIFICATION

Furthermore, coin collecting may be used to diversify an investing portfolio. Traditional financial assets, such as stocks, bonds, and real estate, are susceptible to the same market pressures, resulting in linked risks. Including rare coins in your investment portfolio may help diversify your holdings since their value is not primarily determined by the success of the stock market or other investment vehicles. This diversity may help spread risk and perhaps improve the overall performance of your investing portfolio, particularly during market turbulence.

FINANCIAL PROTECTION

Coins may also be used as a hedge against inflation and economic uncertainty. Coins, unlike paper money, may keep their fundamental worth despite inflation or economic swings. During economic downturns, demand for precious metals and rare coins rises as investors and collectors seek alternative assets that might help them retain their money. "So, if you have precious metal coins, you have made a wise financial decision."

PERSONAL RELATIONSHIP

Coin collection may have emotional significance as well. Many collectors acquire coins as presents or inherit them from family members, providing a personal link to the collection. Coins may be treasured relics that elicit memories and feelings, elevating them beyond the status of mere metal.

Interaction with Others

Coin collecting may also be a social pastime that enables you to meet other people who share your interests. "There are many coin collecting groups on social media, local coin collecting clubs, and even coin shows, conventions, or auctions where you can meet new people and expand your circle of friends."

Relaxation and Enjoyment

Last but not least, coin collecting is a relaxing and enjoyable activity. Searching for pennies, studying them, and arranging them may be a relaxing and satisfying hobby that can help you de-stress and unwind. It may also be a fascinating and exciting pastime that gives you a feeling of success and fulfillment when you add a new coin to your collection or finish a set.

The Metal Content

Coins are constructed of different metals that are reusable and recyclable. The biggest advantage of collecting antique coins is their metal content. Coins are constructed of several metals, including copper, nickel, and zinc. These metals may be melted and utilized in different ways. This facilitates recycling and helps to preserve resources.

The metal composition of coins also influences their worth. Certain coins are more valuable than others because they contain more precious metals. A gold coin, for example, contains more gold than a copper coin. This increases the coin's value and makes it more valuable.

So, if you're seeking an ecologically beneficial activity with monetary rewards, collecting old coins may be for you!

SENSE OF ACHIEVEMENT

Collecting antique coins is a task that may provide you with a feeling of success that can be quite satisfying. When you have an antique coin collection, you give yourself a chance to feel successful in your collecting endeavors.

Every time you add another item to your collection, particularly if it is rare and difficult to obtain, you may have the same happy emotion. This may make the pastime incredibly seductive, and many collectors find themselves becoming lost in it.

Something to Remember

Some coin collections are the consequence of many generations collecting them. If you are a parent or grandparent who has been collecting coins for some time, you may have something to hand on to your children or grandkids.

One of the most valuable things you can do with coins is this. You may leave a legacy that will continue for centuries if you have anything to pass on. Coins have a way of passing down from generation to generation, and having something like this these days is extremely unusual.

Collecting antique coins is a rewarding pastime that may be quite lucrative if you do your research. Furthermore, they all have historical and educational significance, which makes them even more appealing to certain individuals. The metal content may be used, and having a significant collection gives individuals a feeling of achievement. Finally, you may make it a family tradition by passing it on to your children or grandkids. The most essential thing to remember is to enjoy yourself!

Coin collecting has several advantages that extend beyond the basic act of gathering coins. It mixes the pleasures of history and art with the possibility of financial gain, making it a really satisfying and enjoyable pastime for both novice and experienced collectors. "So, whether you're a new or experienced collector, keep collecting because you never know when your next coin will contain a fascinating story, a beautiful design, and a promising investment opportunity all rolled into one."

CHAPTER 7

WHERE TO LOCATE COINS

METHODS OF LOCATING COINS

There are several methods for collecting coins. The following are examples of common collection themes:

- Country
- Time period

- Coin finish
- Denomination
- Mint mark
- Design theme
- Artist

The Mint produces annual sets based on some of these themes, including uncirculated, proof, and quarter sets, to make it simpler to collect.

Error Coins

The Mint makes errors from time to time. Although the majority of mistaken coins are recycled before they reach the Mint, the ones that do make it into circulation are frequently regarded as valuable. Prior to the development of sophisticated equipment, coins had a range of die, planchet, and striking defects. Here are several examples:

- Off-center hits
- Several strikes
- Overstrikes
- Planchets that have been clipped
- Diets with flaws

More information regarding inaccuracies may be found in numismatic publications and organizations.

Compile Your Collection

Finding and purchasing coins might be an excellent way to increase your collection.

Consider the following before adding a coin to your collection:

- Do you find the coin appealing?
- How gleaming is it? There is no way to restore the luster of a coin.
- Is it broken? Scratches, bag markings, staple marks, and rust can reduce the value of a coin.
- How well-worn is it? The most important aspect in establishing a coin's grade is wear.

PURCHASING AND TRADING COINS

If you can't find what you're searching for in our catalog or Coin Seller Database, you may also browse for coins on:

Banks

Look through a bank's coin rolls.

Collectors

Coins may be traded or purchased independently or via coin clubs.

Coin Traders

Coin traders purchase and sell coins. You might ask an experienced collector for recommendations on reliable sellers.

Coin Displays

Purchase coins at national or regional coin exhibits.

Auctions

Rare and pricey coins are often accessible exclusively via auctions. Before purchasing, check costs to avoid overpaying and confirm an acceptable return policy.

Antique fairs and flea markets

Coins may be discovered at a variety of events, although with less competition, increased pricing or the sale of "problem coins" may occur.

Scales for Grading Coins

The Sheldon coin grading scale is used to estimate the worth of a coin based on variables such as how well it was manufactured, how much wear it has accumulated, and its shine. A coin is given a number ranging from 1 to 70, as well as an adjective such as bad, excellent, extremely fine, or mint condition. The grade is either "MS-70" or "F-15".

FIND A LOCAL COIN DEALER

When looking for a local coin dealer near you, don't pull out your smartphone and type in "coin dealers near you." A little study will go a long way, whether you're going to show him some coins to discover what they are, find out how much they're worth, or sell some coins.

Many of the people listed in Internet search engines under "Coins" are pawnbrokers, junk bullion purchasers, jewelers, and others who do not collect or study rare coins. They acquire your coins at a low price, sometimes for their bullion value. This procedure will almost always end with you being taken advantage of. To protect yourself, take your time and do some research before driving to a coin dealer.

Find an Honest and Knowledgeable Local Coin Dealer

To verify that you're talking with a knowledgeable coin dealer and that the dealer you go to is honest and ethical, you should first review the Professional Numismatists' Guild (PNG) database.

The PNG has extremely strict membership standards. You primarily want to ensure that you have redress if anything goes wrong, and you also want an experienced dealer who has been evaluated by his peers for ethical conduct. These coin merchants have been thoroughly verified to verify their honesty. They are well-versed in numismatics and rare coins. Their reputation is more important to them than earning fast cash from an unwary consumer.

Another Source for Local Coin Dealers Is the ANA

Although I usually advocate PNG Dealers above others since PNG has by far the highest standards, there may be no PNG dealer in your area. In this scenario, you might look for someone in the American Numismatic Association's (ANA) Dealer Directory.

The ANA also has a code of ethics, so you have some redress if you are sold fake coins or coins that have been incorrectly graded, but the ANA is nowhere near as diligent as the PNG in resolving conflicts when people are unable to reach an agreement directly. The ANA, on the other hand, is far more likely to have a local coin dealer in your city.

Local Dealers are Found at Coin Shows and Coin clubs.

If you can't locate a local coin dealer via the PNG or ANA, look into local coin groups in your region. The ANA maintains a Coin Club

Directory, and you may also try searching Google for phrases such as "Your-City Coin Clubs" or "Your-City Coin Shows."

Of course, you may replace "your city" with the city where you reside or the largest adjacent city while searching. Many local coin clubs host monthly events at which dozens of dealers set up tables and purchase and sell coins. If you are unable to locate a coin show, contact a local coin club to check if there are any coin shows or dealers nearby. There will almost certainly be someone interested in your coin collection.

Many coin sellers may not have a physical shop. Competition has gotten stronger in the era of the Internet, and profit margins have shrunk. Having a physical shop is a costly luxury, and the coin dealer must sell a sufficient number of coins to cover the costs. With so much money invested in the shop, the coin dealer has a strong interest in preserving his reputation.

Finding Local Coin Dealers Through Other Sources

If none of the previous approaches provide results in locating a local coin dealer, the Yellow Pages, but not the online version, is the next place to look. Examine the advertising in the "Coin Dealers" section of the physical book. You can often tell if a dealer is a good option just by glancing at his advertisement. Advertisements that state, "We buy junk jewelry and bullion," are not a suitable option. You want advertising that states things like "Specializes in US Coins" or "Gold Coins" or makes some mention of specific coins rather than merely wanting to acquire coins for scrap metal prices.

Last Resorts for Finding a Local Coin Dealer

If none of the previous approaches provide any results in your area, broaden your search to include local newspapers or online local news outlets. In classified advertisements, there is generally always a "Coins" area where individuals advertise to purchase and sell coins privately.

Call a handful of these people and strike up a conversation with them. Some of them are part-time dealers or collectors who sell on eBay or at local events on the side, and they like assisting the beginner or non-collector. But beware: some of these men may also be immoral!

If you must choose this path, be prepared. Get a copy of the Red Book and check up on your coins yourself first, so you know what's worth the most, and don't allow these folks to "cherry-pick" you. Sell everything or nothing at all, and never sell anything if it doesn't seem right!

FINDING A TRUSTED COIN DEALER

Coin collecting has been a popular pastime for hundreds of years, dating back to the Renaissance. Many individuals are driven to this activity primarily to collect significant coins, such as rare coins, gold coins, mint mistake coins, and historical coins. There are many of these coins that are precious, but there are also numerous recreated and counterfeit coins that resemble their more expensive counterparts but are worth considerably less. This is why it is critical for serious coin collectors to understand how to choose a reliable coin store, whether they are trying to sell their coins or purchase more for their collection.

It is easy to be duped by fake coins and coin dealers attempting to take advantage of inexperienced collectors. Before you go to a coin store to purchase or sell coins, make sure you consider the following factors to guarantee that the dealer is legitimate:

Research Their Experience

Important Pointers for Choosing a Reliable Coin Dealer In general, the longer a coin dealer has been in business, the more knowledgeable they should be about appraising rare and precious coins. Many coin collectors see their purchases as an investment and, as a result, seek the assistance of a reputable and competent coin dealer to ensure that they get the correct information. Going into a coin shop and speaking with its pros is the best way to gather the information you need to establish a coin buyer's experience and skill. The coin dealer should be asked the following questions:

- How long have you been in operation?
- What are your particular areas of expertise?
- Is your coin business a member of the Professional Numismatists Guild (PNG) or the American Numismatists Association (ANA)?
- What is the American Numismatic Association (ANA)?
- Do you have a physical location? (You meet coin dealers at coin shows.)
- Do you have any industry partners?

The answers to these questions will offer you a far better understanding of the coin dealer's expertise and specialty. Membership in the PNG or ANA is a plus since it indicates that the coin dealer has established an adequate degree of skill and ethics in order to be admitted to these organizations. It is also a positive indicator for a coin dealer to have industry partners since it demonstrates respect and consistency with their colleagues.

Check For Real Assets

It is essential for a coin dealer to have legitimate assets so that you can be certain that they will be in business for the foreseeable future. If the store is brimming with genuine coins and other treasures, it is a solid indication that the company is financially secure. It is also conceivable that the valuables in the business are being sold on consignment, implying that the coin dealer does not genuinely own these goods. It is important to determine how long the coin dealer will be in business in order to avoid being duped by a coin dealer who will soon go out of business.

Assess Their Reputation Among Peers

Assessing a coin dealer's reputation among others in their business is an excellent technique to determine their credibility. If coin dealers are unethical or untrustworthy, they may develop a negative reputation among their colleagues, making it prudent to avoid them. If you know other coin collectors, ask them about their experiences with various vendors. This will provide you with further information about a coin dealer's reputation.

Assess Their Ethics

When evaluating a coin dealer, ethics are critical since it is all too easy for a dealer to take advantage of those who do not know what their coin collections are worth. Membership in the PNG or other similar organizations demonstrates that the coin dealer follows the ethical standards required to be accepted for membership. Ethical coin dealers will always examine each of your coins and present you with a reasonable estimate based on their current market value.

Determine Your Recourse for Disputes

It is important to investigate your options for resolving any disagreements for your own safety. A coin dealer who is not a member of the PNG or any comparable organization is not held to any standards and may be difficult to work with in the event of a disagreement. To resolve a disagreement, PNG members agree to go through an arbitration procedure each time a complaint is brought up. Working with a PNG-member coin dealer with a solid reputation may spare you the bother of filing a lawsuit against a non-member coin dealer.

Here are some more easy guidelines to help you assess if a coin trader is trustworthy:

- Reputable coin dealers should provide free assessments with no strings attached.
- A financial offer for your coins should be matched with an evaluation of your coin collection.
- Many trustworthy coin dealers will visit your house or business to appraise your coins.

FINDING RARE COINS WITH A METAL DETECTOR

If you're a metal detectorist, you're surely aware that one of the most thrilling things to discover is a rare coin. But how can you improve your chances of locating one?

Research the region's history: Before you begin metal detecting, learn about the history of the place you'll be seeking. Look for ancient homesites, schools, and parks where coins may have been lost or thrown.

Use a smaller coil: A smaller coil might assist you in detecting tiny things, such as coins. This is particularly beneficial when looking at regions where there is a lot of rubbish or waste.

Look for signals in the appropriate frequency range: The frequency range of certain metal detectors may be adjusted. Set your detector to a frequency that would most likely detect coins, such as 12 kHz to 15 kHz.

Identify precious coins: Research particular markings, dates, and mint marks to learn how to identify valuable coins. This might assist you in recognizing a precious coin when you come across one.

Join metal-detecting groups or online forums where you may connect with other coin seekers to network. They may provide advice and recommendations, as well as share their own discoveries.

You can improve your chances of discovering rare coins with your metal detector by following these recommendations.

CHAPTER 8

ESSENTIAL TOOLS FOR COIN COLLECTING

I f you want to invest in rare coins, you need to consider purchasing a few instruments to get started. Having this important equipment on hand helps safeguard your collection while enabling you to securely examine each coin.

COIN HOLDERS, FOLDERS, AND ALBUMS

It might be tempting to keep your unusual coins in items you already have, such as a cigar box or Ziploc bag. It is nevertheless essential to keep your coins in specifically designed coin holders, folders, and albums. Coin collecting supplies retain uncommon coins in their original state while also allowing you to inspect the coins in your collection without destroying them. We suggest that you avoid using plastic or PVC holders since they tend to break down over time and stick to coins, lowering their value.

MAGNIFYING GLASSES AND LIGHTS

Many coins contain subtle, sometimes fading characteristics that affect their worth significantly. A magnifying glass and a portable light will allow you to examine a rare coin more closely before purchasing or selling it. These instruments make coin inspection simpler on the eyes and enable you to analyze them more clearly. To view the features of the coin clearly, we suggest investing in a decent triplet loupe. This will allow you to accurately assess the condition of your coins. It may be tough to grade coins on your own at first, so when purchasing rare things, always work with a trustworthy coin dealer.

PROTECTIVE GLOVES

Dirt, oils, and residues on your hands may react with the metals in rare coins and harm them over time. As a result, protective gloves are required to keep coins safe while handling them. Choose gloves made of high-quality cotton since plastic and other materials are more likely to damage the surface of a coin. Egyptian cotton gloves are a fantastic option and can be bought at cheap prices online. Although the cotton gloves will protect your money, it is always a good idea to hold your coins on the edge to avoid any surface difficulties.

SOFT CLOTHS AND PADS

Coins may be damaged by dropping them or sliding them over harsh surfaces in the same way that your hands can. Before handling your rare coins, place a soft pad or microfiber towel on the table. A pad will help reduce the likelihood of a coin rolling off the table and onto the floor. Avoid using any objects with rough or abrasive surfaces that might harm the coin's condition.

Because of heightened global economic instability, now is an excellent time to start diversifying your portfolio by investing in rare coins and bullion. We buy, sell, and evaluate rare coins and bullion consisting of gold, silver, platinum, and other precious metals at Atlanta Gold & Coin Buyers. Call (404) 236-9744 now to schedule an appointment at our Atlanta office.

15 FUNDAMENTAL COIN COLLECTING TOOLS

- Databases
- Lighting
- Magnifying glass
- Gloves
- Viewing pad
- Coin books

- Coin holders
- Ruler
- Display boxes and cases
- Safes
- Digital scale
- Digital caliper
- High-end or digital microscope
- High-quality digital camera
- Coin cataloging software

Each of these instruments is a valuable addition to any collection. If you're on a tight budget, start with the cheapest goods and work your way down. You may buy additional technical instruments as your coin collection expands and gets more advanced. The applications of these tools are discussed further below.

WHAT DO YOU NEED TO BEGIN COLLECTING COINS?

There is no one solution to that question since each coin collector serves a unique function.

Coins are intriguing to look at and collect for a youngster. Experienced collectors adore coins and conserve and display them in different formats for the enjoyment of others. A dealer, on the other hand, may go above and beyond what a collector does to conserve and show coins since the coins are a source of cash.

Each of these techniques requires a unique set of circumstances. Each is a natural evolution as well. A dealer most likely began admiring or collecting coins as a youngster, and this passion blossomed into a pastime, leading them to begin buying and selling coins. They eventually became a dealer, proficient in the art of negotiating, coin evaluation, and pricing.

However, it all likely began with a child's curiosity about coins, which needed relatively few tools or equipment.

The same idea applies to adults who are just starting out with coin collecting. Unless the adult inherits a coin collection, there isn't much coin collecting equipment they require initially. However, as the interest grows, so does the need for tools.

At its most basic, coin collecting necessitates:

- Being able to get coins for your collection
- Understanding the coins you are collecting
- Methods and instruments for handling and storing coinage
- A way for securely storing or presenting the currency

You have all you need if you can obtain the coins, comprehend what you have, and conserve, exhibit, and promote your collection. Having the right tools, on the other hand, makes each of those needs more achievable for a committed collector.

The following is a list of some fundamental coin collecting tools, as well as other equipment that may be useful if your collection expands past the hobby stage.

COIN COLLECTING TOOLS

1. Databases

The first tool is simple yet necessary. This is due to the fact that the method of obtaining coins varies, particularly depending on the worth of the coin in question. There are various methods for obtaining collectible coins:

- Examine all of the coins in your possession for uncommon varieties.
- Ask family members if they have any collectible coins (offer a loan if they don't want to part with them permanently).
- When family members get changed, instruct them to hunt for valuable coins.
- Visit coin exhibitions and dealer shops.
- Coins may be purchased online.

Once you have your coins, you must identify them and value them. If they're in circulation, they're probably not worth much more than face value. If you have unique coins, you should record them and give them the correct values. This is why every coin collection requires the following lists, which should preferably be preserved in a computerized format:

- List of trustworthy merchants
- List of coins available for loan to help you start your collection.
- List of your coin collection
- Schedules for any coin exhibitions that you choose to attend
- Pricing and authenticity reference materials

Setting up a spreadsheet with tabs for each list is the simplest method to create a tool for swiftly analyzing the information on each of those lists. This way, you can immediately access any of the lists, and as your collection grows, you may add new categories as required.

2. *Lighting*

The necessities continue with illumination. You will need lights to view your money properly. Unless you only acquire uncirculated coins in pristine condition, you will need to check what you have.

Identification may be hampered depending on the coin by:

- Dates and other characteristics are obscured by dirt and filth.
- Coin wear and tear (for example, the dates are faint because they have been worn away)
- Trauma damage to coins (the coins are scraped, dented, gouged, and so on).
- Small details that are difficult to see with the naked eye
- Shadows generated by insufficient illumination
- In each scenario, enough illumination is required to correctly identify what you have.

The Light Source Specifications

Fluorescent illumination is often too soft and may obscure flaws or minor details on a coin. The same is true for "natural" lighting; the ideal illumination to have is halogen, especially a 75-watt incandescent bulb. This provides sufficient illumination to view imperfections, ridges, mint features, and any damage on the coin.

3. *Magnifying Glass*

A magnifying lens is just as crucial as good illumination. It aids in the authentication of coin condition and grade, as well as the identification of characteristics that are not visible to the human eye.

You should have three different kinds of magnifiers. You don't need them all while you're just starting out but bear in mind that as your collection expands, you'll need to buy the more costly alternatives.

The first kind is a standard portable magnifying glass. The glass should have a 1.5-to-4-inch diameter with a second, stronger lens inserted in it. The focal length of the base lens should be between 2x and 4x. The secondary lens should have a magnification of 5x to 7x.

If possible, you should also get a sewer magnifier with foundation clamps so you can examine your coins hands-free. This also allows you to examine the coin with both hands.

If your collection develops large enough, you'll want to invest in a jeweler's loupe with a magnification capability of 10x to 15x.

4. Gloves

Coin surfaces, while being composed of metal, are particularly vulnerable to grime as well as the oils and acids on your hands. Gloves assist in keeping your money safe. You should always wear them while dealing with coins that:

- Are in pristine condition
- Are they uncirculated?
- Have a memorial picture or symbol.
- Have an especially clean or shiny face

Several kinds of gloves or finger protection are advised. They are, in order of appropriateness, as follows:

- White soft cotton gloves
- Latex gloves without powder

- Nitrile rubber gloves
- Cots for your fingers

Powder-free latex gloves - a non-reactive coating for your fingertips that is readily cleaned or disposable - are self-explanatory.

Nitrile gloves are a kind of rubber that is very flexible, sensitive, and chemically resistant. They are often blue in hue.

Finger cots are constructed of latex, nitrile rubber, or vinyl and cover one or more fingers. You should only use finger cots if you have no other option since the coin cannot contact unprotected regions of your hands.

Why Does This Matter?

Many people recognize the necessity for hand protection while handling mint condition or uncirculated coins, but many don't understand why it's also a good idea to take the same measures with less valued coins.

The oils and acids on your hands, on the other hand, leave deposits on the surface of whatever they touch, regardless of its worth. These deposits may discolor and even destroy the faces of coins. They also facilitate the accumulation of dirt and debris on coins.

5. Viewing Pad

A coin is robust but not indestructible. It may scrape or dull if dropped on a hard surface. While this is less important for coins in circulation, it is very important for coins that are no longer manufactured.

Uncirculated and mint edition coins have such polished face plates that even dropping them on a table will reduce their value, and sliding them over a table can scar them.

When inspecting coins, it is ideal to lay them flat on a soft surface, such as a cotton pad or soft washcloth. The padding will preserve the coin and prevent it from rolling or sliding on a hard surface. This is especially critical if you are presenting the coins to several individuals outside of any casing.

6. Coin Books

A beginning coin collector may benefit much from two sorts of books. The first is the 'US Coins Red Book,' which is a complete reference to US government-minted coins. The 'Official American Numismatic Association Grading Standards (often known as an ANA Grading Guide) is the other.

All American coins are described and valued in the Red Book. It is the official US coin mintage price guide. Each item also includes a history of the coin as well as a description of its physical attributes.

The ANA Grading Guide explains how the grade of a coin is decided. It has a full explanation of every US coin ever produced. You may use it to evaluate your collection - or a coin you want to sell or purchase - and receive an indication of what to anticipate in terms of value.

7. Coin Holders

Most coin collectors begin with a box or drawer in which they place their valuable coins for safekeeping. As their collection increases and becomes more expensive, they will obviously want to keep their coins in a method that protects them, offers information about them, and enables them to be shown and evaluated.

The essential purpose of a holder is to prevent a coin from being struck, slid, scraped, rubbed against other coins, or dropped and damaged. Another advantage of a coin holder is that it makes it simple to find coins to gift. There are several varieties of coin holders.

Among the many coin carriers are:

- Envelopes made of paper
- Pouch for coins made of plastic
- Sleeves made of 2 × 2 cardboard or vinyl
- Plastic tubing
- Booklets for coin collection
- Coin capsule made of plastic

Any of them will be enough to safeguard your coins. Many collectors acquire preferences for one kind over the others, so it's important to try them all and discover what you like. Most collectors and dealers keep circulation, ungraded coins in coin tubes. Coin booklets usually show one side of the coin and some information about it beneath.

The Air Tite coin capsules are circular, translucent plastic casings into which a coin is placed. Once in place, the front of the capsule latches shut along with the back. These coin carriers are available in a variety of styles.

When your coin collection becomes particularly valuable or contains rare coins, you will most likely migrate valuable coins into a coin 'slab.' A coin is placed in a slab by a third-party grading organization. The slab contains information about the coin as well as its grade. Most collectors and dealers would want to see pricey coins in slabs if you ever sell them.

8. Ruler

When you initially start coin collecting, you won't need a ruler, but it will come in helpful when your collection becomes more complicated, especially if you collect foreign coins. Verifying the size of foreign coins and certain American coins is one approach to prevent purchasing counterfeits. Because a metal ruler might scratch the coins, use a plastic ruler.

9. Display Boxes and Cases

Display boxes or cases can come in a variety of shapes and sizes. The most basic are tiny boxes that may be sealed and used to keep your money safe. The most opulent are hardwood boxes with a glass viewing window, lights, and a presentation platform for exhibiting the currency in a public place where anybody interested may see it.

The kind you need, or if you require both, is determined by your coin collecting goals. If you want to use it sparingly, boxes are probably your best choice. A display case is a preferable option if you want to show off your coin collection to anybody who comes by.

10. Safes

As your coin collection grows in value, you should consider storing it in a safe. You should, at the very least, store your most expensive coins in a safe or lockbox. If you utilize a safe, shelving is essential for keeping your collection organized. If you don't care about the organization, a regular security safe will suffice.

If you have a lot of expensive coins, you should look into bigger safes. A gun safe with storage is one possibility. These are tough to break into and feature a number of shelves big enough to hold cartons, capsules, or pamphlets. They are also often backed by a guarantee as long as they are utilized properly.

11. Digital Scale

If you want to purchase or sell coins, you will need a digital scale to ensure that the coins you are purchasing are genuine. A scale may also aid in the identification of an erroneous coin or clad coin, which is useful for coins from years with both clad and solid metal coins.

When the United States abandoned silver quarters during the year before and at the start of the transition, certain quarters were struck that were solid metal coins with a high silver content, while others were silver clad. Obviously, knowing the distinction is critical if you want to purchase or sell these particular coins.

12. Digital Caliper

This is an essential size gauge. It is useful for determining the diameter of a coin. Coins that are not the correct diameter are most likely one of the following:

- Extracted from a collar
- Had a wide strike
- Minted with an incorrect planchette

The value of these coins is determined by the sort of issuance the coin holds. Some will only manufacture coins worth their face value. Others have the ability to improve the worth of a coin.

13. High End or Digital Microscope

A powerful microscope is required to grade a coin. The zoom range is typically 10x to 45x, allowing you to inspect the coin at practically any degree of magnification you'll ever want. These microscopes may also be used to check mint conditions, seek traces of circulation, or look for distinctive features on a particular coin.

14. High-Quality Digital Camera

This is vital for insurance purposes if your coin collection is valuable. It may also be beneficial if you decide to sell coins online. Some individuals photograph their coin collection using their iPhones, but this may not capture the amount of detail or documentation you want.

Each coin imaged should have the following information:

- Date and time stamp of the photo's capture
- Front and rear views of the coin
- Photograph of any coin-related information
- To avoid picture manipulation, use a digital watermark.

Each picture should also be duplicated three times:

- One for your security.
- One for the insurance firm
- One generic collection of photographs for easy reference

15. Coin Cataloging Software

Using software built for this purpose is another option to validate and verify the scope of your collection. Coin cataloging software allows you to record the identifying information and images of each coin. It's also useful for insurance reasons if you have a significant coin collection.

It's also useful if you ever want to sell your collection. Having all of the paperwork in one location, complete with images, is valuable to savvy buyers since it saves them a lot of time if they acquire your collection. It is also a method of verifying everything in your collection if they dispute it after gaining control of it.

This sort of software also keeps track of all purchases, sales, and profits from coin sales. It will also have a reference database to enable proper coin identification. Some coin cataloging software will also keep track of price and sales data from major dealers or auctions.

COIN APPLICATIONS

Smartphones have transformed almost every part of our lives, so it stands to reason that they will do the same for collectors. Apps may assist a coin collector not just in keeping organized but also in managing a coin collection or guaranteeing that the coin price for every transaction is correct.

The best coin collecting apps include:

- Allow coin documentation and cataloging (compatibility with some coin cataloging software)
- Provide coin statistics such as minted totals each year, incorrect coin information, and so on.
- Provide you with coin prices based on several major markets and grades.
- Assistance with coin identification

Every collector will benefit from the tools on this list. You'll need reference materials, magnification tools, and good lighting to get started. While these are necessary for any collector, the additional tools will make it simpler to organize, show, secure, and sell your coins, allowing you to get the most out of your collection.

CHAPTER 9

PRESERVE AND PROTECT:
MAINTAINING THE LONGEVITY OF YOUR COIN COLLECTION

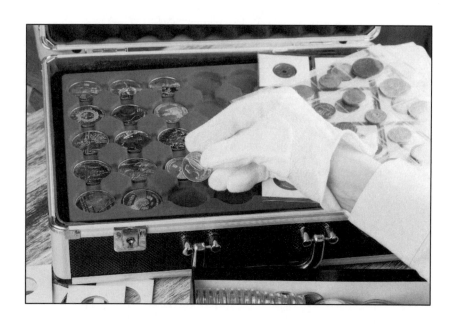

It is essential to properly care for coins in order to retain the quality and worth of a coin collection. Improper cleaning or storage may cause damage to the coin's surface, lowering its value and potentially affecting its look. Use the proper cleaning processes and keep the coins in the proper containers to preserve the beauty and life of each piece in a collection.

CLEANING A COIN

Uncirculated coins should never be cleaned in general. Cleaning tools with abrasive chemicals may discolor a coin, and wiping or polishing leaves microscopic scratches on the surface. Beginners who begin their collections with circulating coins sometimes discover that their purchases seem filthy or boring. Because circulating coins are often damaged, it is appropriate to polish them gently:

- Hands should be properly washed to eliminate extra oils and dirt.
- Warm water should be placed in a small plastic container. A modest quantity of mild detergent should be added.
- Fill a second container halfway with distilled water to use as a rinse.
- Make a drying station out of a nice blanket or towel.
- Immerse the coins in the water one at a time, carefully touching both sides with your fingers. Work from the center of the coin outward.
- Rinse the coin under running hot water.
- Swish the penny in the distilled water to eliminate the chlorine from the tap water.
- Using the drying station, air dries the coin. If distilled water was not used, pat the coin dry carefully.
- Before keeping coins, make sure they are absolutely dry.

It is essential to handle coins one at a time throughout the cleaning process so that they do not come into touch with one another.

Furthermore, eliminating oxidation from a coin might reduce its value. Toning refers to the change in hue that occurs as a result of a coin's natural age. No dips, polishes, or chemical treatments should be used on a coin to preserve the toning.

PROPER TECHNIQUES FOR THE LONGEVITY OF YOUR COIN COLLECTION

Properly preserving and maintaining your coin collection will ensure that it remains in excellent shape for future generations. It was once remarked, "We are not the owners of our coin collection, but the stewards of these items for future generations of coin collectors." Showing your collection to other coin collectors, family, and friends is one of the most enjoyable aspects of coin collecting. One of the greatest gifts we can offer future generations is to preserve these riches.

Coins are works of art that convey stories. Coins are pieces of history in your hands. These tales and history are meant to be remembered on coins for future generations. With the proper equipment and resources, you will be able to preserve and secure the coins in your coin collection. If you follow these rules, you will be on the right route to properly conserving your coins and safeguarding them for future generations.

HANDLING COINS PROPERLY

Improper handling is the most prevalent cause of coin damage. Always hold a coin by its edge so that your skin's oils and acids do not come into touch with the coin's faces. To reduce the danger of harming your coins, wash your hands before handling them. Also, be careful to place the coin on a soft fabric or pad. The coin will not be harmed if you drop it.

If the coins are in a specific container, such as one from the United States Mint or one from a grading agency, you should keep them in their holders or capsules. Taking a coin out of a particular holder might also reduce its worth. Because they want to keep their coin collections in a specific book or case, some collectors may remove their coins from their coin holders. Learn how to correctly handle your coins so you don't damage them and may enjoy them for years to come.

COIN COLLECTING SUPPLIES FOR THE BEGINNER

Every coin collector will need a variety of coin collecting equipment in order to properly store their coin collections and appreciate the effort they have done in creating their coin collections. The coin materials you need will be determined by how you like to keep and safeguard your coin collection. You'll also need to consider the expense of the materials you'll need to house your collection.

Coin holders, files, albums, magnifying glasses, suitable lighting, books, gloves, and a nice surface to work on are all included. Beginning collectors will just need the basics; however, intermediate and experienced collectors will need a broader range of equipment and materials. Every coin collector, however, will need a magnifying lens or loupe. It should be no more than a tenfold increase.

Intermediate and Advanced Coin collecting Supplies

As coin collectors gain knowledge and expertise, the coin collecting materials they need will evolve. You will go from collecting coins based only on their date and mint mark to additional areas such as die variants and mistake coins.

To ensure that a coin is genuine and not a forgery, you'll need coin collecting gear, including a digital scale, a digital caliper, a stereo microscope, a natural daylight bulb, a high-quality digital camera, and coin cataloging software. The more advanced your coin collecting materials need to be as your collection increases.

Flat Clinch Stapler

You will need to staple the 2 × 2 cardboard coin holders shut if you use them. When using a conventional office stapler, the staple will be crimped below the holder, with two bumps emerging from the rear of the holder. You can flatten these ridges using a pair of needle-nose pliers, but you risk scratching the coin.

A simpler alternative is to purchase a flat clinch stapler, which forces the staple under the holder into the cardboard, preventing the staple from protruding from the rear of the cardboard holder. This will protect another coin in a cardboard holder next to it from being damaged by the staple.

Whatever kind of stapler you use, additional caution must be given while stapling the cardboard coin holder shut. Stapling too near to the coin may cause it to get damaged. This damage will cause a decrease in value.

Magnifier and Light

To examine your coins correctly, you will need suitable lighting and a magnifying to assist you in seeing them better. Incandescent lighting is the greatest kind of lighting. Fluorescent illumination is excessively soft and mild, and it may conceal severe flaws from you. In contrast, halogen lights are overly bright and may draw undue attention to tiny flaws on your coin. A basic desk light with a 75-watt incandescent bulb is perfect. If you can't locate an incandescent bulb, try an LED bulb with a complete color range.

Some coin collectors choose to utilize two types of magnifiers. The first kind is a hand-held lens, which typically measures 1.5 to 4 inches in diameter and has a magnification capability of 2X to 3X. This form of glass gives an entire view of the coin's elegance and eye appeal. A jeweler's loupe with a magnification capability of 10X to 15X is appropriate for a more detailed examination of a coin's surface.

Books

The U.S. Coins "Red Book" (A Guide Book of United States Coins) and The Official American Numismatic Association Grading Standards of United States Coins (ANA Grading Guide) are the first two publications that every coin collector should obtain. The Red Book is the official price reference for US coinage. It gives a short history and description of every coin ever produced in the United States. The ANA Grading Guide, which includes a full explanation of every United States coin and how a grade is obtained, is another vital reference book.

Gloves

Your skin's oils and acids may harm the delicate surface of any coin. Gloves are particularly important while handling uncirculated coins with flawless surfaces. Wear gloves to protect your coins from the oils and acids on your fingertips. Soft cotton gloves are preferred by the majority of professional numismatists. Powder-free latex or nitrile gloves, which may be obtained at any pharmacy, are an alternative to cotton gloves.

Pad or Soft Cloth

Finally, many coins are harmed when they are dropped upon hard surfaces. As a precaution, always work on a soft pad or fabric that will cushion your coin in case you drop it. Furthermore, the cushion or cloth will keep your currency from rolling about on the floor and further harming it.

COIN FOLDERS AND COIN ALBUMS

Whether you are a novice coin collector or a seasoned collector with years of expertise, you may choose to store part of your collection in a coin folder or coin album. Coin collectors of any budget may choose from a broad range of alternatives.

Both choices have the benefit of arranging your collection in a certain order. This helps you to easily determine which coins you are lacking and must get. Coin folders are cheap and ideal for novices. Intermediate and advanced collectors may wish to invest in coin albums to secure their precious coin collections. These folders and albums, however, may not offer enough security for particularly rare and costly coins for expert coin collectors.

Coin folders and albums are a practical method to store and preserve your coin collection while also displaying it for your friends or pleasure. These coin supplies vary in price from a few dollars for a coin folder to more than $40 for a personalized coin book.

Each approach has benefits and drawbacks. The major benefit of these storage solutions over coin holders is their small size and capacity to keep a high number of coins in a single album or folder. A tiny coin album may be the perfect choice if you have limited room in your safe or safe deposit box.

If you have valuable coins that have been encapsulated by a third-party grading firm, you will not want to break them open and place them in a coin folder or album. The easiest way to keep them safe is to keep them in their unique enclosed container. This is proof of grade and authenticity. The guarantee is null and invalid if the coin is broken out of the holder.

Coin Folders

Using cardboard coin folders is one of the simplest and least costly solutions to safeguard and organize your coin collection. There are numerous manufacturers, but they all give the same amount of security for your coin collection.

This option offers new collectors a low-cost method to get started in coin collecting. Their straightforward form and basic layout give a clear roadmap for beginner collectors to chronicle their coin collecting experience.

Publishers make coin folders by cutting circular holes on cardboard that fit the coin perfectly and keep it in place. Each hole includes a label with the date or description of the coin that goes there. As you construct a full collection of coins in that folder, this information will help you plan your coin collecting adventure.

Unfortunately, the design of these coin folders only enables you to see one side of the coin. Furthermore, the coin is exposed to the environment, as well as probable fingerprint damage from others touching your money.

Coin Albums

Coin albums are comparable to coin folders in storage capacity, and they enable you to organize and safeguard your coin collection at the same time. They are more costly than coin folders, but they offer various benefits.

For starters, they enable you to see both sides of the coin while they are contained inside the album. Second, a plastic insert covers both sides of the coin, protecting it from fingerprints and unintentional damage. Some manufacturers charge an extra fee for a cardboard slipcase that protects the cover and the edge of your coin album. Furthermore, unlike coin folders, coin albums do not have a page restriction of three or four. Some coin albums may accommodate up to 200 coins.

However, coin albums suffer from the same drawback as coin folders. For example, if the album is constructed of a substance that includes tiny levels of sulfur or acids, they might leak out of the album page and destroy your coin. As a result, to preserve the integrity of your coins, keep them in a cold, dry area.

Caution: Toned Coins

One of the reasons coin collecting became popular in the early 1900s was the advent of coin boards. These were enormous sheets of cardboard that were built similarly to coin folders but did not fold into practical sizes.

Unfortunately, at the time, the production procedures employed acids in the cardboard and glue. These acids leached out of the substance over time, causing the coins contained therein to tone. Although true corrosion was uncommon, the toning of copper and silver coins exhibited bright hues at times and unattractive black blotches at others. Acid-free materials are being used by coin folders and album producers.

Warning: PVC Damage

Coin albums, unlike coin folders and coin boards, employ plastic covers to safeguard the coins. Again, early producers produced plastic slides from polymers that included PVC (polyvinyl chloride) to soften and make the material more malleable.

What they didn't know was that the PVC would leak out of the plastic and attach to the coin's surface over time. This chemical procedure creates an unsightly green slime on the coin, making it unappealing. It may really harm the coin if left on it for a lengthy period of time. By following some basic steps, you may remove the PVC residue from the coin without causing any damage.

Caution: Slider Marks

As coin collecting supply producers became aware of the issues related to PVC-containing polymers, they made efforts to address them. They not only began utilizing PVC-free polymers, but they also conducted further testing to guarantee they were composed of inert ingredients that would not chemically degrade the coin.

The disadvantage of this method was that the polymers were hard and unyielding rather than soft and flexible. The edges of the plastic slides that covered the coins might rub across the coin and produce minor scratches known as hairlines or slider marks if collectors were not cautious while removing or replacing the plastic slides that covered the coins. These are often located on the coin's highest points, although they may also harm the coin's field.

PROTECT YOUR COIN COLLECTION BY CHOOSING THE BEST COIN HOLDERS

Coin holders enable you to keep your coins safe from harm caused by mistreatment or other environmental variables. There are several coin holders available to help you arrange your collection, each with its own set of benefits and drawbacks. You will be able to locate coin holders that match your coin collecting demands, ranging from economical 2 x 2 coin holders to pricey, encapsulated coin holders offered by third-party grading agencies.

If you leave your coins unprotected or keep them in the improper sort of coin holder, they might get damaged. This damage has the potential to severely lower the value of your coins or, in the worst-case scenario, render them useless. Each form of coin holder offers varying degrees of security, as well as various benefits, downsides, and related expenses.

When selecting a coin holder, you should consider the following factors:

- The Size of the Holder: Some coin holders are quite elegant but take up a lot of room. If you attempt to put your coin collection in a secure vault, it may take up more space than you have.

- Cost: Some coin carriers may be rather pricey. Some coin holders might be more expensive than the coin they retain. However, if you want to keep your coin collection constant, this may be your only choice.

- Coin holders are available in a number of designs. Some are extremely cheap and are intended to retain coins just momentarily. Others might be rather costly or even custom-made.

- Durability: The coin holder's durability is a crucial aspect. If you have cheap coins and need a cheap solution to keep them, a cardboard container could be the way to go. A valuable coin, on the other hand, should be placed in an enclosed container from a third-party grading firm that ensures its authenticity and grade.

2x2 Coin Holders

A 2x2 coin holder (sometimes known as a 2-by-2) is a two-inch-by-two-inch square cardboard holder. A Mylar plastic sheet is bonded to the interior of the holder, which has one or more circles cut out. When folded over and stapled close, the coin is held securely and can be seen on both sides while being protected from fingerprints and environmental damage.

Other sizes available include 1.5 inches for smaller coins and 2.5 inches for larger coins. Another brand glues the holder shut with adhesive. The main drawback of self-adhesive holders is the time it takes to put them together. To prevent corrosion or discoloration on your coins, you must also ensure that the self-adhesive coin holders are acid-free.

Benefits include the ability to write identifying information on the holder, the capacity to arrange and reorganize coins on 2x2 pages (see below), and the ability to see both sides of the coin.

Disadvantages: When removed from the holder, staples may damage the coin, and they are not airtight.

2 x 2 Pages

2x2 pages enable you to arrange your 2x2 cardboard holders in any manner you like. Furthermore, they will allow you to keep and examine your collection in any three-ring binder accessible at local office supply shops. Purchase non-PVC-based papers and three-ring binders. Otherwise, the environment may harm your coins as PVC leaches out of the plastic and into the environment around them.

They are also available in 1.5-inch and 2.5-inch cardboard holder sizes. These pages may also include coin flips (see below). To prevent bulging staples on the rear of the holder, use a flat clinch stapler. When inserting or withdrawing the coin, they may damage the plastic 2 x 2 sheets. Furthermore, if the staple is not flat, it might damage the coin next to it.

Benefits include a low cost, the ability to organize and rearrange your collections, and the opportunity to display both sides of your coins.

Disadvantages: For larger coin collections, it might become quite cumbersome.

Coin Flips

Coin flips are little plastic containers with two pockets. One pocket holds the coin, while the other may hold a little piece of cardboard describing and cataloging your coin. The most typical size is 2" by 2", although they also exist in 1.5" and 2.5" sizes for smaller coins and 2.5" for bigger coins.

These are most typically used by coin dealers because of their compact form and ability to be housed in long cardboard boxes that can be labeled and arranged. On the paper insert, coin dealers may also put inventory numbers, identifying information, and pricing. A coin collector might use this to learn more about a coin before acquiring it.

Advantages: The coin can be readily withdrawn without causing harm, there is a vast space for description/catalog information, it is small, and it is inexpensive.

Disadvantages: It may be constructed of PVC, which may cause harm to your money. Coins may fall out by mistake. It is not the finest way to show off your coins.

Hard Plastic Coin Holders

Rigid plastic coin carriers provide some of the greatest coin protection. Most are constructed of inert plastics like polystyrene. Unlike cardboard 2x2 holders and coin flip, stiff plastic holders are designed to accommodate a specified coin size. They are available in a variety of shapes and sizes and may carry individual coins, uncirculated sets, proof coins, and whole collections. Capital Plastics is the leading maker of bespoke holders.

Advantages: Superior security, a large range of alternatives and styles, the ability to see both sides of the coin, and the coin cannot simply slip out.

Disadvantages include bulky storage, high cost, and no place to record identifying information.

Encapsulated Coins

Your coin will be best protected if it is encapsulated. A strong, inert plastic casing that is acoustically sealed to offer a practically airtight environment protects the coin. A soft, inert plastic insert suspends the coin inside the plastic shell, preventing it from moving or vibrating and causing harm. In addition, an expert verifies the coin's authenticity and offers a professional assessment of its grade.

Advantages include the best possible protection, assured authenticity, and expert grading.

Cons: Expensive (average of $30 or more per coin). The only way to get the coin out is to smash the holder.

Coin World Premium Coin Holders

Coin World's Premium Coin Holders resemble the enclosed coin holders (shown above). Some folks call them "DYI (Do It Yourself) Slabs." They provide many of the same safeguards, such as a hard plastic shell and a soft, inert insert to securely contain the coin. However, they are not acoustically sealed and are thus not considered airtight. Furthermore, they have not been validated or graded by a competent numismatist.

Advantages: Some of the greatest coin security available, as well as the ability to store identifying and catalog information within the holder. Furthermore, the holders are not permanently sealed. This enables you to check the coin and then replace it in the holder.

Disadvantages: Moderately priced (around $1 to $2 per holder).

Coin Tubes

Coin tubes are used to store and preserve rolls of coins from the elements. They are available in a range of shapes and sizes, including hard clear plastic round tubes and opaque plastic square tubes.

Benefits: The ability to keep a big number of coins in a little amount of space.

Disadvantages: Moderate cost ($.50 to $2 per tube), coins may be damaged by vibration, and coins must be removed to be seen.

SLABBED COINS OFFER THE BEST PROTECTION

For valuable and rare coins, the only logical option is to encapsulate them utilizing a third-party coin grading service's encapsulation method. You not only receive the nicest coin holder money can buy, but you also get a guarantee that the coin is legitimate and an expert numismatist's judgment on the coin's quality. Encapsulating your coins, on the other hand, is not confined to exceptionally precious coins. A valued coin that is neither uncommon nor precious but has substantial emotional value may be worth spending at the expense of having the coin encapsulated by a competent third-party grading agency.

The word "slab" refers to any sort of holder used by third-party grading services after properly authenticating and grading your coin. There are several benefits to sending your coins to third-party grading agencies. One of the most important reasons to hire a third-party grading service is to have your coin verified by a competent numismatist. The second most significant benefit is that your coin will be housed in the strongest and most durable coin holder money can purchase.

Third-party Grading Services

Third-party grading services first appeared in the late 1970s and early 1980s to give a professional numismatic judgment on a coin's grade while also ensuring its authenticity. During this period, many investors realized the value of buying rare coins. During this period, coin values were typically rising, which drew the attention of numerous investors. Unfortunately, many individuals began calling themselves "coin dealers" and selling over-graded coins at high rates to persons inexperienced with coin collecting and grading methods. As a consequence, many individuals suffered substantial losses and were disillusioned with the coin collecting pastime.

Third-party grading firms use experienced numismatists who analyze each coin for authenticity and offer their professional judgment on the coin's overall grade. The coin is then sealed in a clear plastic container to protect it from environmental and physical harm. Because the coin is suspended inside the holder using an inert plastic insert, these holders will not harm it. Furthermore, you cannot remove the coin from the holder without harming or ruining it. These tamper-evident containers serve as an additional barrier to counterfeiters who target coin collectors.

The introduction of third-party grading services helped to stabilize the coin collecting industry, particularly for rare and valuable coins. Buyers were no longer reliant on the opinion of the same person that was selling the currency. A third party with no inherent interest in the transaction may now offer a professional and impartial judgment on the coin's grade and, as a result, it's worth. Furthermore, counterfeit coins were recognized and removed from the market more readily. However, instances of counterfeit third-party holders carrying counterfeit coins have lately surfaced.

Slab Holders

Slab holders are primarily designed to retain rare and valuable coins for lengthy periods of time. The inert plastic insert that comes into touch with the coin's edge is specifically designed not to react with the coin's metal. This includes physical damage to the coin and ensuring that the plastic insert does not produce any gasses that might cause discoloration or corrosion on the coin's surface.

The outside casing is composed of clear durable plastic. Although this plastic does not come into direct touch with the coin's surface, it is comprised of an inert substance that will not produce gases or react with the coin's metal surface in any manner. Furthermore, the outside plastic housing is made of high-quality plastic that is optically clear and will not discolor over time.

Finally, within the coin holder, they insert a label stating the coin's denomination, year of minting, other identifying qualities, and the professional numismatist's judgment on the coin's grade. The coin is then sonically sealed, creating a nearly airtight barrier between the top and bottom halves of the outer housing. Any attempt to remove the coin or tamper with the grade given would be seen on the coin's holder.

Why Slab Coins

Experts strongly advise submitting any precious or uncommon coins to one of the top-tier third-party grading agencies (PCGS, NGC, ANACS). You not only get an expert numismatist's assessment of the coin's grade and authenticity, but you also get the finest quality holder to safeguard it. Remember that even the smallest fingerprint might lower the value of a rare coin. Most significantly, these holders safeguard the coin from physical harm if it is dropped upon a hard surface unprotected.

The expense of getting your coins slabbed is the major downside. Submitting a coin to a third-party professional coin grading firm might cost anywhere from $10 to $30 or more. However, the value you get in return might be priceless. Finally, when the time comes to sell your coins, whether by yourself or your heirs, there will be no confusion about how to value a coin since its kind and grade have already been established by a competent numismatist.

The top third-party grading providers also offer smartphone applications. PCGS and NGC have both released applications that allow you to scan the barcode on the slab's label using your phone's camera. It will use the Internet to query a database in order to acquire crucial information for the coin you are holding in your palm. It will also provide retail pricing value information for your currency if it is accessible. This may then be used to estimate how much your currency could sell for on the open market.

Alternatively, some purist coin collectors believe that putting a coin in a slab is essentially "entombing" it, preventing you from properly appreciating the coins in your collection. The ability to handle a raw coin (one that is not in a holder or album) enables you to thoroughly explore the coin's surfaces. The slab's plastic may generate reflections that might potentially disguise and be in perfection.

Although this is the greatest approach to conserve individual coins, keep in mind that there are extra measures to protect, maintain, and store your complete coin collection.

SAFELY STORING YOUR COIN COLLECTION

Putting your money in coin holders and albums is the first step in assuring their safety. But where you keep your coins is as crucial. Other than misuse, the most common causes of coin damage include humidity, excessive heat or cold, acids, salt, chlorine, and air pollution.

You will be able to take further measures in identifying where the safest spot to keep your money if you understand how each of these elements might harm them. People who live near the seaside must exercise extra caution owing to excessive humidity and salt levels in the air. No matter where you reside, you must take the required steps to safely keep your coin collection. As a result, future generations will benefit from your coinage.

Coin collections have a long and rich history, and in order to preserve that heritage, you must keep your coins properly. When it comes time to sell your coins, properly preserved coins will be worth more and offer more money to your heirs.

Mints produce coins from metal, and with the exception of gold, most will respond unfavorably to a number of environmental variables. Copper and silver are two of the most popular metals used in coinage. These elements are also among the most chemically reactive. If you know who your adversary is, you may devise a defensive strategy to defend your collection.

The Causes of Damage

Although most metal is a sturdy element, a number of circumstances may have a detrimental influence on the condition of your coins. Many coin collectors store their coins for extended periods of time without ever inspecting them. Checking on the state of your coins in storage on a regular basis is one of the greatest strategies to prevent harm from occurring.

Humidity

The most dangerous enemy of a coin is humidity. Copper and silver coins are among the most frequent metals used in coin manufacture. Unfortunately, when these two metals come into touch with water, they will react chemically. Water vapor is present in varied degrees all around us and can infiltrate almost everything. Unfortunately, this is one of the most difficult environmental sources of coin damage to avoid. Some businesses promote coin holders as "airtight," although this is not a guarantee.

Cold and Heat

Heat by itself does not always cause coin damage. Heat, on the other hand, shortens the time it takes for a coin to be harmed by other environmental conditions, including humidity, acids, and air pollution. Cold, on the other hand, may harm the delicate surface of uncirculated coins when moisture condenses into liquid water and deposits itself on the coin's surface.

Acids

Acids are derived from a number of sources. The most prevalent source of acid is coin collection materials made of normal paper and cardboard that were acid-treated during the manufacturing process. These acids will leach out of the paper or cardboard over time, causing toning and tarnish, particularly on copper and silver coins. Acids may also be emitted by packing adhesives. Another source of acid is wood furniture and common home products such as cleaning solutions and cooking gasses. Avoid putting your coin collection in a cupboard that also houses cleaning products or other chemicals.

Chlorine

Chlorine triggers a chemical reaction that degrades the look of your coins. This might vary from mild ugly toning to corrosion-causing pits in the coin's surface. One of the biggest causes of this is flips manufactured of PVC (polyvinyl chloride)-containing plastic. Furthermore, gases from a hot tub or pool might infiltrate into the space where your coin collection is kept.

Air Pollution

Air pollution not only harms our health, but it also harms the health of our coin collections. Air pollution is mostly a concern in congested metropolitan settings, where haze from automobiles may concentrate and enter neighboring buildings. Although attempts have been attempted to decrease the number of toxic gases emitted by cars, they might still exist in sufficient quantities to destroy a coin. Avoid putting your coins near a garage or a storage place containing petroleum products.

Improper Handling

The most avoidable sort of coin damage is caused by improper handling. Directly touching a coin with your fingers may create deposits of acids and oils that harm the surface. Dropping a coin on a hard surface may also inflict permanent damage, lowering the coin's value. Always use appropriate coin-handling practices. This includes using soft cotton or nitrile gloves to handle your cash. Always work with your coins on a soft pad or cloth.

Best Storage Solutions

Unfortunately, there is no way that can completely secure your coins. However, you may pick the correct atmosphere and coin supplies to preserve your coins from any harm while they are in storage.

Choose the Right Coin Holder, Album, or Folder

Storing your collection in a box, container or just placed into a dresser drawer can result in substantial currency damage. The first step in preserving your coin collection is to properly store it in a coin holder, coin album, or coin folder. Coin albums and folders, in addition to safeguarding your coins from physical harm, let you arrange your collection by providing a slot for you to insert your coin within the album. The folders and albums are labeled with dates, mint markings, and other information to help you catalog your coin collection at the same time.

Location

The ancient real estate cliché "location, location, location" is true. Where you keep your collection is just as essential as how you keep it. Your general rule of thumb should be, "if the environment is comfortable enough for a person, it will probably be satisfactory for your coins."

Extremes such as a cellar (cold and damp) or attic (hot and harsh) must be avoided in order to maintain your coin collection in the best possible shape. The greatest place to put it is in a den or bedroom. Additionally, avoid storing your currency holders, folders, and albums in an area where cooking oils and moisture may easily infiltrate.

If you live near the water or sea, you must take extra steps to protect your coins from damage caused by the damp and salty climate. Copper coins are particularly vulnerable to environmental degradation caused by moisture and salt in the air in coastal regions.

Safe Deposit Box

A safe deposit box at a bank is one of the safest locations to keep your coin collection. Unfortunately, this is also the most costly option. Bank vaults are built to keep thieves and firemen out. Bank vaults are composed of a substance that emits water vapor, which keeps the temperature in the vault low in the event of a fire. Some water naturally escapes over time. As a result, your collection would be in an extremely humid atmosphere. Placing a silica gel pack inside your safe deposit box will absorb the water vapor. Change it at least twice a year to keep it fresh and absorbing as much water vapor as possible.

A Safe for the Home or Office

A safe for your home or business to keep your coin collection is a less costly choice. There is no recurring yearly cost with a safe, as there is with a safe deposit box. Home and business safes, unfortunately, are made of the same material as bank vaults. You should also use a silica gel pack to absorb humidity and protect your money from harm.

You might also consider investing in a properly placed alarm system. This will safeguard your house, family, and currency collection from different attacks. Intruders, fire, flood, and dramatic weather fluctuations are among the hazards.

Metal Bookcase or Cabinet

As wood ages, the coatings, glue, and the wood itself may leak dangerous compounds into the atmosphere surrounding your coin collection. Although not as secure as a safe, a lockable metal cabinet will keep your collection safe since it does not have the difficulties associated with wood. Because metal attracts moisture in the form of condensation, be cautious where you place your metal cabinet. Taking humidity from the air and putting it on your coins might be disastrous. Protecting, conserving, and keeping your coin collection correctly can guarantee that your coins are appreciated by future generations.

SAFES, SECURITY, AND COIN COLLECTION INSURANCE

Nobody likes to consider their coin collection stolen or destroyed. These things, however, are a reality of life. With adequate coin collection security, you may reduce the likelihood that a criminal will take your precious coin collection or that it will be damaged in a fire. If one of these things occurs, having appropriate insurance to cover the expense of replacing your beloved coin collection might alleviate your sorrow.

Additionally, attempting to preserve a certain amount of anonymity and secrecy might aid in the protection of your collection. Attending a coin club meeting where other collectors share their tales and the coin collecting journey is an excellent opportunity to meet new people. People outside the coin collecting community, on the other hand, may have no other interest in your collection except to steal it.

CATALOGING YOUR COIN COLLECTION

One feature that distinguishes "coin collectors" from "coin accumulators" is that they are obligated to catalog their coin collections. An essential component of coin collecting is keeping a written record in the form of a catalog. If you have insurance coverage to safeguard your coin collection in the event of a loss, you will need to produce a complete inventory of your collection when filing a claim. You will also know precisely what coins you have and what coins are needed to complete a certain series in your coin collection. Nothing is more annoying than buying a coin just to discover that you already own that coin.

CHAPTER 10

GETTING FAMILIAR WITH NUMISMATIC LANGUAGE:
UNDERSTANDING KEY TERMINOLOGY

The study of coins and money, as well as coinage and coin-like artifacts, is known as numismatics. Numismatics is derived from the term numismatic, which means "of coins." It was taken from the Latin term Nomisma, which means currency and was borrowed from French numismatiques in 1792.

The word "numismatics" was first used in English in 1829. At the beginning of any subject, correct terminology usage is critical. The study of coinage resulted in the development of its own language. To introduce the topic, some of the fundamental words and vocabulary of numismatics are employed.

COIN ANATOMY AND PARTS

Coins, like any other object, possess distinct parts and components. Understanding the various elements of a coin's anatomy is essential for accurate description and identification. Let's explore the key terms related to coin anatomy:

Obverse

The obverse, also known as the "heads" side, is the front face of a coin. It typically features a prominent design, such as a portrait, symbol, or emblem. The obverse often contains inscriptions identifying the issuing authority, the denomination, or the historical figure depicted.

Reverse

The reverse, or the "tails" side, is the back face of a coin. It provides a complementary design to the obverse and often features national symbols, commemorative images, or other relevant motifs. The reverse may also include inscriptions such as the coin's country of origin, its face value, or commemorative text.

Edge

The edge refers to the outer perimeter or border of a coin. It serves as a protective barrier, shielding the main surfaces from wear and damage. The edge can be plain, featuring no particular design, or it can be decorated with various elements such as reeding (parallel grooves), lettering, or ornamental patterns.

Rim

The rim is the raised area around the edge of a coin. Its primary function is to protect the main surfaces from wear and damage by creating a barrier between the edge and the rest of the coin. The rim also adds an aesthetic dimension, framing the design elements on the obverse and reverse.

Field

The field refers to the smooth, flat surface of a coin's obverse or reverse. It encompasses the area surrounding the central design elements and is often left blank to provide contrast and emphasize the primary motifs. The field provides a backdrop against which the main design elements stand out.

Legend

Legends are inscriptions or text present on a coin. They serve to provide essential information such as the country of origin, the denomination, or historical context. Legends can be found on both the obverse and reverse of a coin and may vary in size, style, and location depending on the specific design.

COIN GRADING TERMS

Coin grading is a crucial aspect of coin collecting. Grading allows collectors to assess the condition and quality of a coin, providing an indication of its desirability and potential value. Understanding the terms used in coin grading will empower you to make informed decisions and accurately describe the condition of your coins. Let's explore some common coin-grading terms:

Mint State (MS)

Mint State refers to a coin that has never been in circulation. These coins retain their original mint luster, with no signs of wear, damage, or toning. Mint State coins are often highly sought after by collectors due to their pristine condition.

About Uncirculated (AU)

About Uncirculated coins show minimal signs of wear. They may have slight traces of friction on the highest points, but the majority of their original luster remains intact. AU coins are considered to be in excellent condition and are highly desirable among collectors.

Extremely Fine (XF)

Extremely Fine coins display only slight wear on the highest points of the design. The majority of the original details and luster are preserved. XF coins are considered to be in above-average condition and are sought after by collectors.

Very Fine (VF)

Very Fine coins exhibit moderate wear on the high points of the design. Despite this wear, the main design elements and inscriptions remain clear and easily readable. VF coins are still in good condition and are valued by collectors.

Fine (F)

Fine coins show considerable wear, with the design elements appearing flattened. While some details may be worn or obscured, major design features and inscriptions are still distinguishable. F coins are considered to be in average condition.

Very Good (VG)

Very Good coins exhibit significant wear, with flattened details and major design elements showing signs of merging. Despite the wear, the inscriptions and primary motifs are readable, allowing for identification. VG coins are still collectible but are considered to be in below-average condition.

Good (G)

Good coins are heavily worn, with little remaining detail. Major design elements are still discernible, but finer details may be obscured. G coins are generally considered to be in low-grade condition.

MINTING AND PRODUCTION TERMINOLOGY

Understanding the terminology related to coin minting and production processes provides insight into how coins are created and the factors that contribute to their uniqueness. Let's explore some key terms related to minting and production:

Die

A die is a metal tool engraved with the design elements of a coin. Dies are used in the striking process to impress the design onto blank metal discs called planchets. Each coin typically requires two dies—one for the obverse and one for the reverse.

Planchet

A planchet is a blank metal disc prepared to be struck by the dies and transformed into a coin. Planchets are typically made of base metals or precious metals, depending on the coin's composition and intended use.

Mint Mark

A mint mark is a symbol or letter(s) that indicates the mint that produced a particular coin. Mint marks can vary between countries and mints. They provide valuable information for collectors, allowing them to identify coins produced at specific mint facilities.

Proof Coin

A proof coin is a specially produced coin with highly polished dies and planchets. The striking process for proof coins involves multiple strikes, resulting in a sharp, mirrored finish and exceptional detail. Proof coins are carefully handled and stored to maintain their pristine condition.

Error Coin

An error coin is a coin that contains an unintentional mistake or anomaly during the minting process. These errors can occur due to issues with the dies, planchets, or striking process. Error coins are unique and highly sought after by collectors due to their rarity and distinct characteristics.

COLLECTING AND PRICING TERMINOLOGY

As you delve deeper into the world of coin collecting, you will encounter specific terms related to the collecting process and the valuation of coins. Understanding these terms will enable you to navigate the collecting landscape with greater confidence. Let's explore some essential collecting and pricing terminology.

Key Date

A key date refers to a coin that is scarce or rare within a specific series. Key dates are often associated with a particular year or mint mark and are highly sought after by collectors. The rarity of key date coins contributes to their higher value and desirability.

Mintage

Mintage refers to the total number of coins produced for a specific design, date, and mint mark combination. The mintage figure provides insight into the relative rarity of a coin. Coins with lower mintages are generally considered more scarce and may command higher prices among collectors.

Bullion Coin

A bullion coin is a coin made from precious metals, such as gold or silver. Bullion coins typically have a high metal content, and their value is based primarily on their weight and purity. Bullion coins are often sought after by investors and collectors alike for their intrinsic value.

Face Value

Face value refers to the nominal value of a coin, typically indicated on the coin itself. This value represents the legal tender value assigned to the coin by the issuing authority. However, the face value of a coin may differ significantly from its intrinsic or collector value.

Market Value

The market value of a coin represents its current price or worth in the collector's market. Market values are influenced by various factors, including rarity, demand, condition, historical significance, and prevailing market conditions. Market values can fluctuate over time as collectors' tastes and market dynamics evolve.

CHAPTER 11

GRADING YOUR COINS:
EVALUATING THE CONDITION AND QUALITY OF YOUR COINS

C oin grading is the process of assessing a coin's grade or condition, which is one of the most important aspects in evaluating its worth. The grade of a coin is normally decided by six criteria: strike, preservation, luster, color, beauty, and, on rare occasions, the country/state in which it was produced. A variety of grading systems have been devised. Certification services grade coins professionally for a charge.

A "grade" describes the look of a coin. A coin's grade is determined by five factors: strike, surface preservation, shine, coloring, and eye appeal. Grading is subjective, and even specialists might differ on a coin's grade.

The grading of US coins has developed over time into a system of finer and finer grade differences. There were originally just two grades: new and worn. This was changed to a letter grading system, beginning with Basal State (also known as Poor (PO)) and progressing through Fair (Fr), About or Almost Good (AG), Good (G), Very Good (VG), Fine (F), Very Fine (VF), Extremely Fine (EF), Almost or About Uncirculated (AU), Uncirculated (Unc), and Brilliant Uncirculated (BU). At the time, Gem Uncirculated was basically similar to BU in use. The verbal scores are now accompanied by numerical grades ranging from 1 to 70.

THE IMPORTANCE OF COIN GRADING

Why is coin grading important? Coin grading serves several essential purposes in the numismatic community:

Preservation of History

Proper grading helps preserve the historical integrity of coins by identifying their condition at a specific point in time. It allows collectors to maintain a record of the coin's state and history.

Determination of Value

Coin grade directly influences a coin's value. Higher-grade coins generally command higher prices due to their better condition and rarity.

Market Transparency

Grading provides a standardized system that facilitates transparent transactions among collectors, dealers, and investors. It enables parties to communicate accurately about a coin's condition and value.

Comparison and Appreciation

Grading allows collectors to compare coins of similar grade and appreciate the subtle differences in quality and condition. It fosters a deeper understanding and appreciation for the artistry, craftsmanship, and historical significance of each coin.

GRADING SYSTEMS AND STANDARDS

There are multiple grading systems and standards used in the numismatic community. The most widely recognized and utilized grading systems include:

Sheldon Scale

The Sheldon Scale, also known as the numerical grading scale, was introduced by Dr. William H. Sheldon in 1949. It assigns a numerical grade from 1 to 70 to coins, with 70 representing a perfect coin in Mint State (MS) condition.

American Numismatic Association (ANA) Scale

The ANA Scale, developed by the American Numismatic Association, is a descriptive scale that categorizes coins into various grades, ranging from Poor (PO) to Mint State (MS). The ANA Scale incorporates terms such as Fair (FR), Very Good (VG), Fine (F), Very Fine (VF), Extremely Fine (EF), and About Uncirculated (AU), among others.

Professional Coin Grading Service (PCGS) and Numismatic Guaranty Corporation (NGC) Grading Standards

PCGS and NGC are two prominent third-party grading services that have established their grading standards. Their grading systems are widely accepted and trusted in the numismatic community. These services use numeric grades, with the addition of a "+" or "★" to indicate exceptional quality within a particular grade.

It is essential to familiarize yourself with these grading systems and understand the specific criteria used to assign grades within each system. This knowledge will enable you to communicate effectively with other collectors, dealers, and professionals in the field.

FACTORS AFFECTING COIN GRAD

Several factors influence a coin's grade. Understanding these factors will help you evaluate the condition and quality of your coins accurately. The key factors affecting coin grade include:

Wear and Surface Preservation

Wear is one of the primary considerations in coin grading. The amount and distribution of wear on a coin's high points, such as the design elements and inscriptions, directly affect its grade. The presence of scratches, nicks, stains, or other surface issues also impacts the grade.

Luster and Originality

Luster refers to the reflective quality of a coin's surface. Coins with vibrant luster often receive higher grades. Originality refers to a coin's natural appearance without any signs of cleaning, artificial toning, or alteration. Coins with original surfaces generally receive more favorable grades.

Strike Quality

Strike quality refers to the sharpness and definition of a coin's design elements. Coins with full strikes, where all details are well-defined, tend to receive higher grades. Weak strikes with incomplete or blurred details may result in lower grades.

Eye Appeal

Eye appeal is a subjective factor that considers the overall attractiveness and visual appeal of a coin. Factors such as color, toning, and the overall aesthetics of a coin can influence its grade. Coins with exceptional eye appeal may receive higher grades.

Mint Errors and Varieties

Mint errors, such as planchet flaws or striking errors, can affect a coin's grade. Likewise, certain coin varieties, such as those with different mint marks or die varieties, can impact a coin's grade and value.

Understanding these factors and their impact on coin grade requires experience, knowledge, and a discerning eye. As you gain more expertise in coin grading, you will become adept at assessing these factors and accurately assigning grades to your coins.

DETERMINING COIN VALUES BASED ON GRADE

Coin values are closely tied to their grade. Generally, higher-grade coins command higher values due to their better condition and relative scarcity. The value of a coin is influenced by various factors, including its grade, rarity, demand, historical significance, and market conditions. Here are some general guidelines for determining coin values based on grade:

Research Price Guides

Price guides, such as the Red Book (A Guide Book of United States Coins) or online resources, provide approximate values for coins based on their grades. These guides can give you a general idea of a coin's value within a specific grade range.

Reference Auction Results

Studying auction results can provide valuable insights into the current market value of coins. Auction houses often publish realized prices for coins of various grades, allowing you to gauge the market demand and value for specific grades.

Consult with Experts

Seeking guidance from experienced collectors, dealers, or professional grading services can help you determine the value of your coins more accurately. Experts can provide valuable insights into the nuances of grading and market trends that affect coin values.

Remember that coin values can fluctuate over time as market conditions change. It is crucial to stay informed and regularly update your knowledge of market trends and factors affecting coin values.

CHAPTER 12

THE MAJORITY OF REQUESTED COIN VALUES:
AN OVERVIEW OF COIN VALUATION

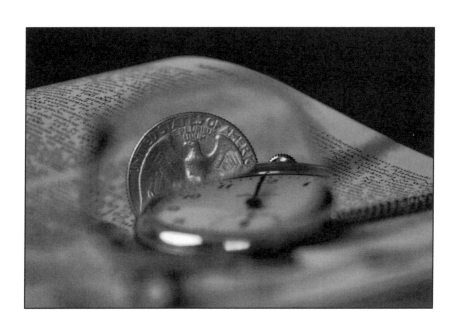

Whether you're new to coin collecting or have been collecting for years, we're all hoping to find one or more that we can sell for a profit! Or if you've been fortunate enough to inherit a huge collection or come across some ancient coins in an attic or estate sale and feel some of the coins are quite valuable.

CONSULTING THE COIN BOOKS AND MAGAZINES

If you're new to coin collecting, you should educate yourself on anything coin-related. Pick up the "Blue Book," an annual printed Guide Book of United States Coins, to discover more about the worth of certain coins you hold.

The Blue Book values are a little closer to the selling prices. The Red Book frequently lists retail values that are greater than what most dealers and coin purchasers would pay.

Inside, you'll discover typical wholesale/retail prices for every coin in the United States based on coin grading. This is a fantastic place to start learning about the worth of your collection. Two of the most important variables in establishing rarity are low mintage and a rare mintmark.

It's crucial to remember that this book only lists the retail value of the coin, not the wholesale value, which is what coin dealers usually pay.

Determining the Value

The value of a coin is determined by three basic factors.

1. Number of Initial Mintage. This refers to the number of coins that were initially struck and were available on the market.
2. Coin Quality. The better the condition of your coin, the more valuable it may be.
3. Demand. The higher the price, the more attractive the coin is to purchasers.

Search for Errors

Tilting a coin under lights might help you uncover faults on the coin that you might not see at first look.

The smallest change may cause a coin to be worth more than its face value. Look for die cracks and missing parts, paying special attention to wording written on the coin and the margins of pictures. Doubled strikes, cracks, and missing parts are other frequent flaws that may improve the value of a coin.

While mistakes are fascinating just because a coin has one, their value is determined by the nature of the defect, and many to most error coins are not highly valued. Furthermore, just because you "saw something on the internet" does not necessarily identify the underlying real-world worth, which is often sensationalized.

To grade and validate, it is better to have errors and values evaluated by a third-party authenticator like NGC or PCGS. These services charge a fee per coin and require members to send in their coins.

Don't Clean Your Coins

Let me say it again: don't clean your coins! This will remove shine and patina from the coin's surface, lowering its value.

A coin's value is not diminished just because it seems filthy. It is also critical to maintain your coins correctly to avoid dings, rim dents, scuffs, and scratches and to keep them as near to pristine condition as possible.

Use coin folders, flips, or albums made of materials that will not harm your coins, such as non-PVC flips. Hold the coin by the rim to prevent your fingers and thumbs from making markings on your face or back from the oils in your hands. Cotton gloves are often used by collectors.

Rare and valuable coins should be handled with extreme care. It could be in your best interest to get them graded by a service.

PRICING FACTORS FOR COINS

Numerous factors contribute to the value of a coin. Understanding these factors is crucial for accurately assessing and determining the worth of your coins. Let's explore some of the key pricing factors for coins:

Rarity

Rarity is one of the most significant factors influencing coin value. Coins that have low mintage numbers from limited editions or possess unique features are considered rare and often command higher prices.

Condition

The condition, or grade, of a coin, plays a vital role in determining its value. Coins in excellent condition, with minimal wear and exceptional preservation, generally fetch higher prices than coins in lower grades.

Historical Significance

Coins that hold historical importance, such as those associated with significant events or periods, often carry higher values. Coins that were part of limited-issue commemorative sets or were minted during specific historical eras may be particularly sought after by collectors.

Metal Content

The intrinsic value of the metal used in a coin can significantly impact its worth. Coins made from precious metals, such as gold or silver, often have higher values based on the current market price of these metals.

Demand and Popularity

The demand for specific coins can drive their prices up. Coins that are highly sought after by collectors due to their design, historical relevance, or rarity may command premium prices in the market.

Scarcity

The scarcity of a coin, beyond just its mintage numbers, can affect its value. Coins that are difficult to find in the market or that have limited surviving examples due to various circumstances may carry higher price tags.

Errors and Varieties

Coins with mint errors or notable varieties can hold significant value due to their uniqueness and appeal to collectors. These coins often attract attention and command higher prices in the market.

Understanding these pricing factors will enable you to assess the value of your coins more accurately. Keep in mind that multiple factors can influence a coin's worth, and their relative importance may vary depending on the specific coin and the current market dynamics.

COIN VALUE GUIDES AND ONLINE RESOURCES

Coin value guides and online resources provide invaluable assistance in determining the approximate worth of coins. These resources offer insights into the market value and pricing trends for various coin types and grades. Some commonly used coin value guides and online resources include:

Red Book (A Guide Book of United States Coins)

The Red Book, published annually, provides comprehensive information on United States coins, including historical background, mintages, and estimated values for different grades. It is a widely recognized and respected resource among collectors.

Online Coin Price Guides

Numerous online platforms offer coin price guides that provide up-to-date values for various coins. These guides often allow you to search by coin type, grade, and other relevant criteria, enabling you to access the most current pricing information.

Numismatic Marketplaces

Online marketplaces dedicated to numismatics, such as eBay, provide a wealth of information on current coin prices. These platforms allow you to search completed listings to see the final sale prices for coins similar to yours.

Coin Dealer Price Lists

Coin dealers often publish price lists that reflect their current buying and selling prices for different coins. These lists can provide insights into the market value of specific coins and grades.

When using value guides and online resources, it is important to remember that they provide approximate values based on market trends and other factors. Coin values can fluctuate due to changing market conditions, demand, and other variables. Therefore, consider these values as a starting point and consult multiple sources to gain a more accurate understanding of the market value of your coins.

APPRAISALS AND PROFESSIONAL COIN VALUATIONS

Appraisals by professional coin experts offer a more precise and personalized assessment of the value of your coins. These professionals possess in-depth knowledge, expertise, and experience in evaluating coins. Here are some key points to consider regarding appraisals and professional coin valuations:

Appraisal Services

Numerous professional coin appraisal services exist, offering specialized knowledge and expertise in coin valuation. These services often charge a fee based on the complexity and number of coins being appraised.

Professional Grading Services

Third-party grading services, such as the Professional Coin Grading Service (PCGS) and the Numismatic Guaranty Corporation (NGC), not only provide grading but also offer a wealth of information regarding the value of graded coins. They employ experts who assess the grade, authenticity, and market value of coins.

Coin Shows and Conventions

Coin shows and conventions provide an opportunity to have your coins appraised by knowledgeable dealers and experts. These events often feature appraisal services and can be an excellent resource for obtaining professional valuations.

Estate Appraisals

If you inherit a coin collection or possess a substantial collection, seeking the services of a professional appraiser specializing in estate appraisals is advisable. These experts can provide detailed appraisals for insurance purposes, estate planning, or selling.

MARKET TRENDS AND DEMAND

Market trends and demand play a crucial role in determining the value of coins. Understanding these dynamics is vital for accurately gauging the worth of your coins. Consider the following points regarding market trends and demand:

Collecting Trends

The numismatic market is influenced by collecting trends, which can shift over time. Coins that align with current collecting interests or themes may experience increased demand and higher values.

Popular Series and Designs

Coins from popular series or featuring iconic designs often attract more attention from collectors. Increased demand for these coins can result in higher prices.

Historical Events and Anniversaries

Coins associated with significant historical events or anniversaries may experience heightened demand and value during corresponding periods. Collectors may seek out these coins to commemorate specific occasions.

Economic Factors

Economic conditions and fluctuations in precious metal prices can impact the value of coins made from gold, silver, or other precious metals. Market conditions and investor demand for these metals can influence the value of related coins.

Rarity and Market Demand

Coins that are both rare and in high demand among collectors can experience substantial increases in value. These coins often generate excitement and competition among collectors, resulting in higher prices.

Monitoring market trends and demand can help you anticipate changes in coin values and make informed decisions about buying, selling, or holding onto your coins. Stay engaged with the numismatic community through forums, publications, and attending coin shows to stay informed about current market dynamics.

CHAPTER 13

COMMEMORATIVE AND OTHER SPECIAL COINS:
A CLOSER LOOK AT UNIQUE AND LIMITED-EDITION ISSUES

I n the world of coin collecting, there is a vast array of unique and limited-edition coins that go beyond regular circulating currency. These coins hold a distinct place in numismatics, representing significant events, honoring historical figures, or showcasing exquisite craftsmanship. By exploring commemorative coins, special editions, mint sets, medals, and tokens, as well as rare and limited production coins, you will gain a deeper understanding of the diverse and captivating world of numismatic treasures.

UNDERSTANDING COMMEMORATIVE COINS

Commemorative coins serve as tangible reminders of important events, anniversaries, or individuals of historical or cultural significance. These coins are often issued by governments, institutions, or organizations to honor and celebrate milestones. Understanding the characteristics and significance of commemorative coins enhances your appreciation for these unique numismatic treasures. Let's delve into some key aspects of commemorative coins:

Commemorative coins often celebrate significant historical events, such as the anniversary of a nation's founding, important battles, or major achievements. They provide a tangible link to the past and serve as enduring tributes to the people and events they honor.

Unique Designs

Commemorative coins typically feature distinctive designs that relate to the event or individual being commemorated. These designs often incorporate symbols, portraits, landmarks, or iconic elements associated with the subject matter. The artistic value and intricacy of these designs make commemorative coins highly collectible.

Limited Mintage

Commemorative coins are typically issued in limited quantities, which adds to their appeal and rarity. The limited mintage ensures that these coins remain special and exclusive, attracting the interest of collectors and investors alike.

Precious Metal Content

Many commemorative coins are minted from precious metals such as gold, silver, or platinum. These coins not only carry historical or cultural significance but also possess intrinsic value based on their metal content. Precious metal commemorative coins can be highly sought after by collectors and investors.

Legal Tender Status

While commemorative coins may hold higher value due to their historical or artistic significance, they often maintain legal tender status. This means that, in addition to their collectible value, they can be used as currency in their respective countries of issue.

Collecting commemorative coins allows you to delve into specific historical events, pay tribute to extraordinary individuals, and appreciate the craftsmanship and artistry captured in these unique numismatic creations.

SPECIAL EDITIONS AND MINT SETS

In addition to commemorative coins, special editions and mint sets offer collectors an opportunity to acquire unique and well-crafted numismatic treasures. Let's explore these special editions and sets in more detail:

Proof Sets

Proof sets are specially produced coins that exhibit exceptional quality and finish. They are struck with highly polished dies and planchets, resulting in sharp details, mirrored surfaces, and frosted designs. Proof sets often include coins of various denominations, providing a comprehensive collection of beautifully crafted coins.

Limited Edition Sets

Limited edition sets are carefully curated collections of coins issued in limited quantities. These sets often feature themes such as Olympic Games, wildlife, or historical periods. Limited edition sets may include coins of different denominations, metals, or finishes, making them highly sought after by collectors.

Commemorative Coin Sets

Commemorative coin sets are collections of coins that honor a specific event, individual, or theme. These sets often include multiple coins with complementary designs, offering a comprehensive representation of the subject matter. Commemorative coin sets can be highly desirable for collectors seeking a cohesive collection focused on a particular theme or historical event.

Special Finish Editions

Special finish editions feature coins with unique finishes or embellishments. These finishes can include selective coloring, gilding, or special surface treatments. Special finish editions enhance the visual appeal and collectability of coins, adding a touch of exclusivity to the collection.

Special edition coins and mint sets provide collectors with opportunities to acquire unique and comprehensive collections. The limited availability, special finishes, and thematic coherence make these coins highly sought after by enthusiasts.

COLLECTING MEDALS AND TOKENS

In addition to traditional coins, collectors often delve into the realm of medals and tokens. While these items may not have official currency status, they hold immense historical, cultural, or personal significance. Let's explore medals and tokens in more detail:

Medals

Medals are metallic objects that are not intended for use as currency but are minted to commemorate specific events, honor individuals, or recognize achievements. Medals often feature intricate designs, artistic craftsmanship, and inscriptions that provide historical context. Collecting medals allows you to appreciate the artistry and historical significance associated with various events and personalities.

Tokens

Tokens are similar to coins but are not issued by governments or central banks. They often serve as substitutes for currency in specific contexts, such as transportation, amusement parks, or trade exchanges. Tokens can be highly collectible, representing a wide range of themes, industries, and historical periods. They offer a unique perspective on monetary history and regional commerce.

Collecting medals and tokens provides a fascinating glimpse into the broader world of numismatics. These items offer unique stories, artistic expression, and historical connections beyond traditional coinage.

RARE AND LIMITED PRODUCTION COINS

Rare and limited-production coins are highly sought after by collectors due to their scarcity and desirability. These coins are often characterized by low mintages, exceptional quality, or unique features. Let's explore some examples of rare and limited production coins:

Key Date Coins

Key date coins are coins that are particularly scarce within a specific series or denomination. These coins often have low mintage numbers or are associated with a specific year or mint mark. Key date coins are highly prized by collectors due to their rarity and the challenge they present in completing a collection.

Error Coins

Error coins are coins that display variations or mistakes during the minting process. These errors can range from misprints and misalignments to double strikes or planchet errors. Error coins can hold significant value due to their uniqueness and appeal to collectors seeking the unexpected and unusual.

Pattern Coins

Pattern coins are trial strikes or experimental pieces created during the design or minting process. These coins often feature unique designs, compositions, or finishes that differ from the standard issues. Pattern coins are highly coveted by collectors due to their rarity and historical significance.

Commemorative Gold and Silver Coins

Commemorative gold and silver coins minted in limited quantities can be highly valuable. These coins often feature intricate designs, precious metal content, and limited availability, making them desirable for collectors and investors alike.

Collecting rare and limited-production coins requires a keen eye, research, and a passion for seeking out exceptional pieces. These coins add a sense of exclusivity and prestige to a collection, showcasing the collector's dedication and discerning taste.

CHAPTER 14

HOW AND WHERE YOU CAN PURCHASE BULLION COINS:
INVESTING IN PRECIOUS METAL COINS

A unique category of coins that serve as investments in precious metals. Bullion coins offer collectors and investors the opportunity to own tangible assets with inherent value. In this chapter, we explore the basics of bullion coins, popular types, how to assess their purity and weight, and where to purchase them from reputable dealers and mints. By understanding the fundamentals of investing in bullion coins, you can confidently navigate the market and make informed decisions.

Bullion coins are minted from precious metals such as gold, silver, platinum, or palladium. Unlike commemorative or numismatic coins, which may carry additional value due to their rarity or historical significance, bullion coins derive their primary worth from the intrinsic value of the metal they contain. These coins are highly sought after by collectors and investors as a means to preserve wealth and hedge against economic uncertainty.

Bullion coins offer several advantages for investors:

1. Intrinsic Value: Bullion coins have intrinsic value due to the precious metal content they contain. This provides stability and inherent worth, making them attractive investments.
2. Liquidity: Bullion coins are recognized and traded globally, offering high liquidity. They can be easily bought or sold in various markets, providing investors with flexibility.
3. Diversification: Investing in bullion coins allows for the diversification of investment portfolios. Precious metals have historically shown a lower correlation to traditional financial assets, providing a potential hedge against market volatility.
4. Tangible Assets: Bullion coins are physical assets that can be held and owned. This tangible aspect appeals to investors who prefer to have a physical representation of their wealth.

Understanding the basics of bullion coins is essential before embarking on your investment journey. The next sections will delve into popular types of bullion coins and the factors to consider when purchasing them.

POPULAR TYPES OF BULLION COINS

Several popular types of bullion coins are widely recognized and sought after by collectors and investors. These coins are known for their high purity, fine craftsmanship, and global recognition. Let's explore some of the most popular types:

Gold Bullion Coins

Gold bullion coins are among the most widely recognized and coveted bullion investments. Coins such as the American Gold Eagle, Canadian Gold Maple Leaf, and South African Krugerrand are esteemed for their high gold content and iconic designs.

Silver Bullion Coins

Silver bullion coins offer a more affordable entry point for investors while still providing exposure to the precious metals market. The American Silver Eagle, Canadian Silver Maple Leaf, and Austrian Silver Philharmonic are popular choices among silver bullion coin enthusiasts.

Platinum Bullion Coins

Platinum bullion coins, such as the American Platinum Eagle and Canadian Platinum Maple Leaf, provide investors with an opportunity to diversify their precious metals portfolio. Platinum's rarity and industrial uses make these coins particularly intriguing to collectors and investors.

Palladium Bullion Coins

Palladium bullion coins, including the Canadian Palladium Maple Leaf and the Russian Ballerina Palladium Coin, have gained popularity in recent years. Palladium's industrial applications and limited supply have contributed to its attractiveness as an investment metal.

Each type of bullion coin has its unique characteristics, designs, and global recognition. The choice of which bullion coins to invest in depends on factors such as personal preference, budget, and market conditions. Conducting thorough research and consulting with reputable dealers can help you make informed decisions.

ASSESSING THE PURITY AND WEIGHT OF BULLION COINS

The purity and weight of bullion coins play a crucial role in determining their value. Understanding how to assess these factors is vital when purchasing bullion coins. Consider the following key points:

Purity

Bullion coins are typically minted in high purity to ensure their intrinsic value. The purity of a coin is usually denoted in terms of fineness. For example, a gold coin with a fineness of .999 means it contains 99.9% pure gold. The higher the fineness, the higher the purity and value of the coin.

Weight

Bullion coins are often minted in standard weights, which can vary depending on the type of metal and the coin's specifications. Common weight denominations include troy ounces, grams, or kilograms. Understanding the weight of a bullion coin is essential for accurately assessing its value.

Mint Mark

Bullion coins are often minted by government or private mints and bear mint marks that indicate their origin. Mint marks can add to the collectability and value of the coin. Familiarize yourself with the mint marks associated with specific bullion coins to ensure authenticity and quality.

When purchasing bullion coins, it is crucial to verify their purity and weight. Reputable dealers and mints provide assurance of authenticity and often provide certificates or documentation that validate the bullion coins' specifications. Be cautious of counterfeit coins and purchase from trusted sources to safeguard your investment.

BUYING BULLION COINS FROM DEALERS AND MINTS

When it comes to buying bullion coins, it is important to choose reputable dealers and mints that offer authentic and high-quality products. Consider the following steps and considerations:

Research Dealers and Mints

Conduct thorough research to identify established and reputable dealers and mints. Look for those with a solid track record, positive customer reviews, and a history of producing or selling high-quality bullion coins.

Verify Authenticity

Authenticity is paramount when investing in bullion coins. Ensure that the dealer or mint you choose has appropriate certifications and guarantees the authenticity and purity of their coins. Look for dealers who are members of recognized numismatic organizations or are accredited by reputable grading services.

Compare Prices

Bullion coins' prices can vary among dealers due to factors such as market conditions, supply and demand, and dealer premiums. Compare prices from different sources to ensure you are getting competitive rates. Be cautious of unusually low prices, as they may indicate counterfeit or questionable quality coins.

Purchase Options

Determine the purchase options available from the dealer or mint. This can include purchasing individual coins, tubes, or sealed mint boxes. Consider your investment goals, storage capabilities, and budget when deciding on the quantity and packaging options.

Secure Storage

Once you acquire bullion coins, ensure you have a secure storage solution to protect your investment. Consider options such as safety deposit boxes, home safes, or reputable storage facilities specifically designed for precious metals.

When purchasing bullion coins, exercise caution, conduct due diligence, and seek advice from reputable sources or experienced collectors. It is crucial to approach bullion coin investments with a long-term perspective and a focus on preserving wealth.

| CHAPTER 15 |

SHOWING YOUR COIN
COLLECTION:
DISPLAY AND PRESENTATION IDEAS

A s a collector, it is not only important to acquire and preserve your coins but also to share and display them in an engaging and visually appealing manner. In this chapter, we will delve into various strategies for organizing and arranging your collection, explore display cases and cabinets as storage options, discuss framing and mounting techniques for individual coins or sets, and provide insights into sharing your collection with others. By implementing these display and presentation ideas, you can enhance the enjoyment and appreciation of your coin collection.

ORGANIZING AND ARRANGING YOUR COLLECTION

Organizing and arranging your coin collection is a crucial step in showcasing its beauty and significance. Here are some tips to consider

Categorize by Country or Region

Group your coins based on their country of origin or region. This approach allows for easy comparison and highlights the diversity within your collection.

Sort by Denomination

Arrange your coins by denomination, such as pennies, nickels, dimes, quarters, or specific currency units. This organization method provides a clear visual representation of the different coin values within your collection.

Chronological Order

Arrange your coins in chronological order, starting with the oldest coins and progressing to the most recent ones. This method showcases the evolution of coinage over time and highlights its historical significance.

Theme-based Displays

Create themed displays within your collection by grouping coins based on a specific topic, such as historical events, famous figures, or cultural motifs. Themed displays add visual interest and allow you to tell compelling stories about your coins.

Customized Coin Albums

Utilize coin albums designed specifically for organizing and displaying coins. These albums often have labeled slots for each coin and provide protection against damage while allowing easy viewing and access.

DISPLAY CASES AND CABINETS

Display cases and cabinets serve as functional and visually appealing storage options for your coin collection. Consider the following aspects when selecting display cases or cabinets:

Size and Capacity

Choose a display case or cabinet that can accommodate your current collection and provide room for future growth. Consider the dimensions, number of shelves or drawers, and overall capacity to ensure sufficient space for all your coins.

Security and Protection

Look for display cases or cabinets with secure locking mechanisms to safeguard your collection. Ensure that the materials used provide protection against dust, moisture, and UV rays, which can cause damage to your coins over time.

Visibility

Opt for display cases or cabinets with clear glass or acrylic panels that offer optimal visibility. This allows viewers to admire your collection without physical contact, reducing the risk of damage or wear.

Lighting

Consider adding appropriate lighting to your display case or cabinet to enhance the visibility of your coins. LED lights with adjustable brightness are ideal for illuminating your collection without causing heat or discoloration.

Accessibility

Choose display cases or cabinets that provide easy access to your coins when you want to handle or examine them. Sliding or removable shelves and drawers facilitate convenient interaction with your collection.

Display cases and cabinets not only protect your coins from environmental factors but also elevate their visual impact. Place your display case or cabinet in a prominent location, such as a study, living room, or dedicated display area, to create a focal point and invite admiration from visitors.

FRAMING AND MOUNTING COINS

Framing and mounting individual coins or coin sets can be an artistic and visually appealing way to showcase your collection. Here are some methods to consider:

Coin Frames

Use specially designed coin frames that encase individual coins or sets. These frames often have transparent windows to allow for easy viewing while providing protection. Coin frames come in various sizes and designs to suit different coin types and display preferences.

Shadow Boxes

Shadow boxes are deep-set frames that allow for the display of multiple coins or a themed collection. Arrange your coins in a visually pleasing manner, ensuring they are securely mounted or encapsulated within the shadow box.

Coin Holders and Capsules

Coin holders and capsules provide individual protection for each coin while allowing for easy viewing. These holders come in different sizes to accommodate various coin denominations and are often made of materials that offer clarity and durability.

Display Stands

Utilize display stands to present individual coins or sets in an upright position. These stands elevate the coins, making them visually striking and easily accessible for closer examination.

When framing or mounting your coins, ensure that the materials used are archival-quality and non-reactive to avoid any potential damage. Additionally, consider consulting professionals or experienced collectors for guidance on the best methods for framing or mounting specific coins.

SHARING YOUR COLLECTION WITH OTHERS:

Sharing your coin collection with others can be a rewarding experience, allowing you to connect with fellow collectors, enthusiasts, and even the broader community. Consider the following avenues for sharing your collection:

Coin Club Meetings

Join local coin clubs or numismatic societies to connect with like-minded individuals. These groups often hold regular meetings, where members can showcase their collections, discuss numismatic topics, and learn from one another.

Coin Shows and Exhibitions

Participate in coin shows and exhibitions, where you can display your collection alongside other collectors. These events offer opportunities to engage with a broader audience, receive feedback, and exchange knowledge.

Online Communities

Engage with online coin collecting communities through forums, social media groups, or dedicated websites. Share photos and information about your collection, seek advice, and participate in discussions with fellow collectors from around the world.

Presentations and Talks

Consider giving presentations or talks about your collection to local schools, libraries, or community groups. Share your knowledge, highlight the historical and cultural aspects of your coins, and inspire others to explore the fascinating world of numismatics.

Donations to Museums or Institutions

Consider donating select pieces from your collection to museums, educational institutions, or historical societies. This allows a broader audience to appreciate your coins and contributes to the preservation and study of numismatic history.

When sharing your collection, maintain proper security measures to protect your coins from damage or loss. Implement guidelines for handling and ensure that any public displays or presentations are conducted in a controlled environment with appropriate security measures in place.

CHAPTER 16

SELLING YOUR COIN COLLECTION:
STRATEGIES FOR MAXIMIZING RETURNS

Whether you are looking to downsize your collection, liquidate your holdings, or simply explore new opportunities, selling your coins requires careful planning and execution. In this chapter, we will discuss evaluating the market and timing your sales, explore selling options through dealers and auction houses, delve into online selling platforms and marketplaces, and provide insights into pricing and negotiation techniques. By understanding these strategies, you can maximize the returns on your coin collection and ensure a successful selling experience.

EVALUATING THE MARKET AND TIMING YOUR SALES

Evaluating the market and timing your sales are crucial factors in maximizing the returns on your coin collection. Consider the following aspects when assessing the market and determining the optimal time to sell:

Research Market Trends

Stay informed about the numismatic market by researching recent trends, price fluctuations, and demand for specific coins or series. Numismatic publications, online resources, and forums can provide valuable insights into market dynamics.

Seek Professional Appraisals

Engage the services of professional coin appraisers or numismatic experts to evaluate the value of your collection. Their expertise and knowledge can help you determine the current market value of your coins and provide guidance on the optimal time to sell.

Consider Economic Factors

Monitor economic indicators such as inflation rates, interest rates, and geopolitical events that can impact the value of precious metals and numismatic assets. Economic conditions can influence buyer sentiment and market demand for coins.

Focus on Collector Demand

Understand the preferences and interests of collectors within the numismatic community. Coins with historical significance, unique designs, or limited mintage often command higher prices due to increased collector demand.

Timing your sales based on market conditions and collector demand can significantly impact the returns on your coin collection. By staying informed and aligning your sales with favorable market trends, you can optimize the selling process.

SELLING TO DEALERS AND AUCTION HOUSES

Selling your coin collection to dealers or auction houses can provide a convenient and efficient way to liquidate your holdings. Consider the following when choosing this selling option:

Research Reputable Dealers and Auction Houses

Conduct thorough research to identify reputable dealers and auction houses with a strong track record and positive reputation. Look for those specializing in numismatic coins and with experience in handling collections similar to yours.

Obtain Multiple Offers

Approach multiple dealers or auction houses to obtain competing offers for your coin collection. This allows you to compare the terms, fees, and selling conditions offered by different entities.

Consignment or Direct Sale

Decide whether you prefer consigning your collection to an auction house or selling directly to a dealer. Consignment offers the potential for higher returns if your coins generate competitive bidding, while a direct sale to a dealer provides a faster and more guaranteed transaction.

Understand Fees and Commissions

Familiarize yourself with the fees and commissions charged by dealers and auction houses. These fees can vary depending on the value and complexity of your collection. Ensure that you have a clear understanding of the costs involved before finalizing any selling agreement.

Negotiate Terms

Don't hesitate to negotiate terms with dealers or auction houses. Depending on the uniqueness and desirability of your coins, you may have room to negotiate fees, commissions, or other aspects of the selling agreement.

Selling to dealers or auction houses offers the advantage of leveraging their established networks, expertise, and marketing capabilities. However, it is essential to choose reputable entities and carefully review the terms and conditions before finalizing any selling agreement.

ONLINE SELLING PLATFORMS AND MARKETPLACES

Online selling platforms and marketplaces provide an increasingly popular and accessible option for selling your coin collection. Consider the following when utilizing online platforms:

Choose Established Platforms

Utilize well-known and reputable online platforms such as eBay, Heritage Auctions, or specialized numismatic marketplaces. These platforms provide a broad reach and a large pool of potential buyers.

Build a Trustworthy Profile

Establish a trustworthy and professional profile on the online platform. Provide accurate and detailed descriptions, high-quality images, and clear terms of sale. Positive customer reviews and a history of successful transactions can enhance your credibility.

Set Competitive Prices

Research recent sales of similar coins or collections to set competitive prices. Consider the condition, rarity, and market demand when determining the listing price. Pricing your coins attractively can generate interest and attract potential buyers.

Utilize Auction Formats

Consider utilizing auction formats on online platforms to create excitement and competitive bidding for your coins. Auctions can help you achieve the best possible price for your collection.

Secure Payment Methods

Ensure that you utilize secure payment methods to protect yourself and your buyers. Platforms often offer secure payment options or recommend trusted third-party payment processors to facilitate transactions.

Online selling platforms provide a global marketplace for your coin collection, allowing you to reach a wide audience of potential buyers.

However, it is important to exercise caution, thoroughly research buyers, and follow best practices for secure online transactions.

PRICING AND NEGOTIATION TECHNIQUES

Setting the right price and employing effective negotiation techniques are essential for maximizing returns when selling your coin collection. Consider the following strategies:

Research Comparative Sales

Research recent sales of similar coins or collections to determine a fair and competitive price. Numismatic publications, auction results, and online platforms can provide valuable pricing insights.

Consider Grading and Certification

Coins that have been professionally graded and certified by reputable grading services often command higher prices. Highlight the grading and certification details of your coins to enhance buyer confidence and justify the asking price.

Be Open to Negotiation

Recognize that negotiation is a common part of selling coins. Be prepared to engage in constructive discussions with potential buyers and consider adjusting the price or terms to facilitate a successful sale.

Highlight Unique Features

Emphasize the unique features, historical significance, or rarity of your coins when marketing them. These aspects can justify higher prices and attract buyers who appreciate the distinct qualities of your collection.

Provide Detailed Documentation

Present detailed documentation, including certificates of authenticity, grading reports, and any historical or provenance information. Thorough documentation adds credibility to your coins and strengthens your negotiating position.

Remember that the selling process may require patience and persistence. Be prepared for potential fluctuations in the market, varying buyer preferences, and the need for ongoing marketing efforts to attract potential buyers.

CHAPTER 17

AVOIDING AND DETECTING COUNTERFEITS AND SCAMS

C ounterfeit coins and fraudulent activities pose significant risks to collectors and investors, compromising the integrity of their collections and jeopardizing their financial investments. In this chapter, we will explore methods for recognizing counterfeit coins, examine security features and anti-counterfeiting measures employed by mints, discuss how to verify the authenticity and credibility of sellers and identify common scams and red flags to watch out for. By implementing these protective measures, you can safeguard your collection and investments in the fascinating realm of coin collecting.

RECOGNIZING COUNTERFEIT COINS

Recognizing counterfeit coins is essential for preserving the integrity of your collection and protecting your financial investments. Consider the following factors when examining coins for authenticity:

Coin Design and Details

Study the design and details of genuine coins to develop a familiarity with their characteristics. Counterfeit coins often exhibit discrepancies in details, such as poor lettering, incorrect alignment, or blurred images.

Weight and Composition

Be aware of the correct weight and composition of genuine coins. Counterfeit coins may have variations in weight or be composed of different metals, leading to noticeable differences when compared to authentic specimens.

Edge Reeding and Inscriptions

Examine the edge reeding, if present, for inconsistencies in size, spacing, or alignment. Inscriptions on the edge should also be scrutinized for accuracy and legibility.

Magnetic Properties

Some coins have magnetic properties due to specific metal compositions. Use a magnet to test for magnetic attraction, as a lack of magnetism in a coin that should be attracted can indicate a counterfeit.

High-Quality Counterfeits

Beware of high-quality counterfeits that may closely resemble genuine coins. These forgeries can be challenging to detect and often require expert examination.

When in doubt about the authenticity of a coin, consult a professional coin dealer or numismatist with experience in counterfeit detection. Their expertise can help you make informed decisions and avoid costly mistakes.

SECURITY FEATURES AND ANTI-COUNTERFEITING MEASURES

Mints around the world employ various security features and anti-counterfeiting measures to protect their coins from fraudulent replication. Familiarize yourself with these measures to verify the authenticity of your coins:

Microprinting

Look for microprinting, which is the use of tiny text or images that are difficult to replicate without sophisticated printing techniques. Genuine coins often have microprinting in specific areas, such as the rim or around detailed elements.

Laser-Engraved Features

Some coins incorporate laser-engraved features that are difficult to replicate accurately. These features may include intricate patterns, micro-engraved text, or holographic elements.

Special Inks and Foils

Special inks or foils can be used to enhance the security of coins. These inks may have color-changing properties or unique visual effects when viewed from different angles.

Raised or Incused Designs

Genuine coins may have raised or incused designs, which provide a tactile element that is challenging to reproduce accurately.

Mint Marks and Minting Techniques

Pay attention to mint marks and minting techniques specific to certain coins. Familiarize yourself with the genuine mint marks and the techniques used by mints to produce their coins.

By educating yourself about the security features and anti-counterfeiting measures employed by mints, you can become better equipped to identify genuine coins and differentiate them from counterfeits.

VERIFYING AUTHENTICITY AND CREDIBILITY OF SELLERS

Verifying the authenticity and credibility of sellers is crucial when purchasing coins to avoid falling victim to scams or counterfeit transactions. Consider the following steps to ensure a trustworthy buying experience:

Research Sellers and Dealers

Conduct thorough research on sellers and dealers before making any purchases. Look for reputable sellers with a track record of integrity, positive customer reviews, and involvement in numismatic organizations.

Check Credentials

Verify the credentials of sellers or dealers. Membership in recognized numismatic organizations, certifications, or affiliations with reputable grading services can serve as indicators of credibility.

Transparent Policies

Ensure that sellers have transparent policies regarding returns, guarantees, and customer satisfaction. Reputable sellers should be willing to provide information about the authenticity of their coins and address any concerns you may have.

Authenticity Certificates

Request authenticity certificates or grading reports for high-value coins. These documents provide an additional layer of assurance and verify the authenticity and condition of the coins.

Professional Grading Services

Consider purchasing graded coins from reputable grading services. Coins encapsulated in tamper-proof holders with detailed grading information offer increased confidence in authenticity and condition.

Exercise caution when dealing with individual sellers or online platforms, especially when purchasing high-value coins. Verify the credibility and authenticity of the sellers before proceeding with any transactions.

COMMON SCAMS AND RED FLAGS TO WATCH OUT FOR

Being aware of common scams and red flags can help you avoid fraudulent activities and protect your collection and investments. Consider the following warning signs:

Unbelievable Deals

Exercise caution when encountering deals that seem too good to be true. Unusually low prices or offers significantly below market value may indicate counterfeit or misrepresented coins.

Pressure Tactics

Beware of sellers who employ high-pressure tactics to rush your decision-making process. Legitimate sellers should allow you sufficient time to verify the authenticity and quality of the coins.

Poor Quality or Misrepresentation

Be wary of coins that appear to be of poor quality or have obvious flaws. Misrepresented coins may be altered, cleaned, or artificially aged to deceive buyers.

Lack of Transparency

Avoid sellers who refuse to provide detailed information about the coins, their origins, or authentication measures. Transparency is essential in establishing trust and credibility.

Absence of Return Policies

Be cautious when dealing with sellers who have strict no-return policies or do not offer guarantees of authenticity. Legitimate sellers should provide reasonable return options and address any concerns you may have.

Remain vigilant and trust your instincts. If something feels suspicious or too good to be true, it is crucial to conduct further research or seek professional advice before proceeding with a purchase.

CHAPTER 18

THE PERFECT TIME TO SELL COINS

Understanding the market cycles, recognizing potential peaks and lulls, leveraging coin auctions, and implementing effective strategies are crucial elements in maximizing profits when selling your coins. In this chapter, we will explore these concepts in detail, providing you with valuable insights and techniques to navigate the market successfully. By mastering the art of timing your sales, you can optimize your returns and achieve the highest possible profitability for your coin collection.

UNDERSTANDING MARKET CYCLES AND TRENDS

Understanding market cycles and trends is fundamental to timing your sales effectively. The numismatic market, like any other financial market, experiences periods of growth, stability, and decline. Consider the following factors when analyzing market cycles and trends:

Research and Stay Informed

Stay updated with numismatic publications, industry reports, online forums, and reputable market analysis sources. This will help you gather information about market trends, historical data, and key events affecting the numismatic market.

Economic Indicators

Monitor economic indicators that can impact the coin market, such as inflation rates, interest rates, and geopolitical events. These factors influence buyer sentiment and purchasing power, directly affecting the demand and prices of coins.

Coin Series and Types

Study the historical performance of specific coin series or types. Some coins may exhibit cyclical patterns of popularity and value. Familiarize yourself with the historical trends of these coins to make informed decisions.

Collector Demand

Understand the preferences and interests of collectors within the numismatic community. Certain coins may experience increased demand during specific periods due to factors like historical anniversaries, special releases, or changing trends.

By researching and understanding market cycles and trends, you can anticipate shifts in demand and price levels, allowing you to time your sales strategically.

RECOGNIZING POTENTIAL PEAKS AND LULLS

Recognizing potential peaks and lulls in the market is crucial for maximizing profits when selling your coins. Peaks represent periods of high demand and prices, while lulls are periods of lower demand and potential price stagnation. Consider the following factors when identifying potential market peaks and lulls:

Historical Data Analysis

Analyze historical sales data, auction results, and price trends for specific coins or series. Look for patterns that indicate periods of increased activity and higher prices, as well as periods of slower market activity.

Rarity and Desirability

Assess the rarity and desirability of your coins. Coins with limited availability, unique characteristics, or significant historical importance are more likely to experience peaks in demand and prices.

Popular Collecting Trends

Stay attuned to popular collecting trends and emerging areas of interest within the numismatic community. Coins related to popular themes or recently discovered treasures may experience increased demand, potentially leading to price peaks.

Market Sentiment

Gauge the overall sentiment within the numismatic market. Positive economic conditions, strong collector interest, or market-wide enthusiasm for certain coins can indicate potential peaks. Conversely, economic uncertainty or negative sentiment may result in lulls.

COIN AUCTIONS AND MARKET DEMAND

Coin auctions can be valuable platforms for selling your coins, leveraging market demand, and achieving optimal profitability. Consider the following aspects when utilizing coin auctions:

Research Auction Houses

Research reputable auction houses that specialize in numismatic coins. Look for auction houses with a strong track record, knowledgeable staff, and a history of successful sales.

Assess Market Demand

Gauge the current market demand for your coins by researching recent auction results and prices achieved. Assess the level of competition for similar coins and identify auctions where there is likely to be strong interest.

Set Realistic Reserves

Set realistic reserve prices for your coins. A reserve price is the minimum price you are willing to accept for your coins at auction. Setting the reserve too high may discourage bidding, while setting it too low may result in undervalued sales.

Marketing and Presentation

Work with the auction house to ensure proper marketing and presentation of your coins. High-quality photographs, accurate descriptions, and detailed provenance information can enhance buyer interest and generate competitive bidding.

Bidding Strategies

Familiarize yourself with bidding strategies used in auctions. Consider bidding increments, proxy bidding, or utilizing a professional bidder to represent your interests and secure the best possible price.

STRATEGIES FOR MAXIMIZING PROFITS

Implementing effective strategies is essential for maximizing profits when selling your coins. Consider the following strategies:

Diversify Your Sales

Explore multiple sales channels to diversify your selling opportunities. Utilize online platforms, direct sales to collectors or dealers, and auctions to reach a broader audience and increase the likelihood of achieving optimal prices.

Consignment vs. Direct Sales

Assess the pros and cons of consigning your coins to an auction house versus selling them directly to collectors or dealers. Consignment can offer the potential for higher returns through competitive bidding, while direct sales provide more control over the pricing and negotiation process.

Patience and Timing

Exercise patience and avoid rushing into sales when market conditions are not favorable. Timing your sales strategically, based on market cycles, trends, and demand, can significantly impact the profitability of your transactions.

Professional Grading and Certification

Consider having your coins professionally graded and certified by reputable grading services. Graded coins often command higher prices due to increased buyer confidence in the authenticity and condition of the coins.

Price Realistically

Set realistic prices for your coins based on market value, condition, and collector demand. Overpricing your coins may deter potential buyers, while underpricing may result in missed opportunities for higher profits.

Networking and Relationships

Build relationships within the numismatic community and establish connections with collectors, dealers, and professionals. Networking can provide access to potential buyers, market insights, and opportunities for mutually beneficial transactions.

CHAPTER 19

DO'S AND DON'TS OF COIN COLLECTING:
TIPS FOR SUCCESS AND PITFALLS TO AVOID

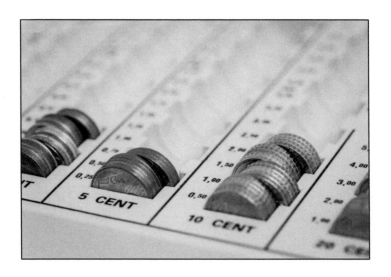

B uilding a solid foundation of knowledge, establishing ethical and responsible collecting practices, avoiding common mistakes and pitfalls, and cultivating a lifelong passion are key factors that contribute to successful and fulfilling experiences in the world of numismatics. In this chapter, we will delve into these aspects in comprehensive detail, providing you with valuable tips and guidance to navigate your coin collecting journey with confidence. By adhering to these principles, you can enhance your collecting expertise, protect your investments, and foster a lifelong love for the art of coin collecting.

BUILDING A SOLID FOUNDATION OF KNOWLEDGE

Building a solid foundation of knowledge is vital for becoming a successful coin collector. Consider the following steps to enhance your knowledge:

Study Numismatic Literature

Immerse yourself in numismatic literature, including books, magazines, and online resources. Read educational materials that cover various aspects of coin collecting, such as history, grading, minting techniques, and specialized coin series.

Attend Coin collecting Events

Participate in coin collecting events, such as coin shows, conventions, and seminars. These gatherings provide opportunities to interact with experienced collectors, dealers, and experts who can share their knowledge and insights.

Join Numismatic Organizations

Become a member of reputable numismatic organizations. These organizations offer educational resources, networking opportunities, and access to exclusive events, fostering your growth as a collector.

Explore Online Communities

Engage with online communities and forums dedicated to coin collecting. Participate in discussions, seek advice, and share your experiences with fellow collectors, expanding your knowledge and understanding of the hobby.

Visit Museums and Exhibitions

Visit museums and exhibitions that showcase numismatic collections. Observe and study the coins on display, appreciating their historical and artistic significance. Museums often provide informative displays and interpretive materials that enhance your understanding of coins.

By continuously expanding your knowledge through research, engagement, and exploration, you lay a strong foundation that enables you to make informed decisions and appreciate the nuances of coin collecting.

ESTABLISHING ETHICAL AND RESPONSIBLE COLLECTING PRACTICES

Establishing ethical and responsible collecting practices is essential for maintaining the integrity of the numismatic community and preserving the value of your collection. Consider the following principles:

Authenticity and Integrity

Prioritize the authenticity of your coins and maintain their integrity. Avoid altering or tampering with coins, and only purchase coins from reputable sources with documented provenance.

Respect for Intellectual Property

Adhere to copyright and intellectual property laws when using coin images or designs for personal or public purposes. Seek permission or utilize licensed images when necessary.

Fair Dealings

Engage in fair dealings with fellow collectors, dealers, and sellers. Be transparent, honest, and respectful in your transactions, adhering to agreed-upon terms and conditions.

Avoid Counterfeit Coins

Take precautions to avoid counterfeit coins by educating yourself on counterfeit detection techniques, buying from reputable sources, and seeking professional advice when in doubt.

Responsible Selling

When selling your coins, provide accurate descriptions and disclose any known issues or repairs. Adhere to ethical practices, respecting the rights and interests of potential buyers.

AVOIDING COMMON MISTAKES AND PITFALLS

Avoiding common mistakes and pitfalls is crucial for a successful and fulfilling coin collecting experience. Consider the following pitfalls and strategies to avoid them:

Impulsive Buying

Avoid impulsive buying by conducting thorough research and carefully evaluating each purchase. Impulsivity can lead to regrets and the accumulation of coins that do not align with your collecting goals.

Overlooking Quality

Pay attention to the quality and condition of coins. Settling for lower-quality coins may hinder the long-term value and appreciation of your collection. Aim for coins in the best possible condition within your budget.

Lack of Focus

Define your collecting goals and focus on specific areas or themes of interest. Avoid becoming a "generalist" collector without a clear direction. A focused approach allows you to build a more meaningful and valuable collection.

Ignoring Market Trends

Stay informed about market trends and collector demand. Ignoring market dynamics may result in missed opportunities or investing in coins that lose value over time.

Inadequate Storage and Preservation

Use proper storage and preservation methods to protect your coins from damage. Neglecting proper care can lead to tarnishing, scratches, or other forms of deterioration that diminish the value and aesthetic appeal of your coins.

By being mindful of these common mistakes and pitfalls, you can make informed decisions, build a focused collection, and avoid potential regrets along your coin collecting journey.

CULTIVATING A LIFELONG PASSION FOR COIN COLLECTING

Cultivating a lifelong passion for coin collecting is essential for sustained enjoyment and fulfillment. Consider the following strategies:

Curiosity and Learning

Maintain a curious mindset and a hunger for continuous learning. Embrace the ever-evolving nature of numismatics and explore new coin series, historical periods, or minting techniques.

Share Your Knowledge

Share your knowledge and passion with others, whether through online communities, local clubs, or educational initiatives. Engaging in discussions and teaching others not only solidifies your own knowledge but also contributes to the growth of the numismatic community.

Regular Reflection

Reflect on your collection and collecting journey regularly. Assess your goals, make adjustments when necessary, and appreciate the progress you have made. Celebrate milestones and achievements, no matter how small.

Attend Coin collecting Events

Attend coin collecting events and gatherings regularly. Interact with fellow collectors, view new collections, and immerse yourself in the energy and enthusiasm of the numismatic community.

Enjoy the Journey

Embrace the joy and excitement that coin collecting brings. Take pleasure in the stories behind each coin, the beauty of their designs, and the connections you make with other collectors. Remember that the true value of coin collecting lies in the journey itself.

By cultivating a lifelong passion for coin collecting, you ensure that the hobby remains a source of fulfillment, inspiration, and intellectual stimulation throughout your life.

CHAPTER 20

DOCUMENTING YOUR COLLECTION:
KEEPING TRACK OF YOUR COINS AND THEIR HISTORY

As a coin collector, it is essential to keep track of your coins and their history to preserve their value and enhance your collecting experience. In this chapter, we will explore the importance of record-keeping, creating a coin inventory, cataloging and describing coins, and researching and documenting their history. By implementing effective documentation practices, you can maintain organized records, uncover fascinating insights about your coins, and create a valuable resource for future reference.

IMPORTANCE OF RECORD-KEEPING

Record-keeping is a fundamental aspect of successful coin collecting. It enables you to track the details, provenance, and value of your coins, ensuring accurate documentation for insurance, appraisal, or future sales. Consider the following reasons why record-keeping is crucial:

Preservation of Information

Documenting your coins preserves valuable information about their acquisition, condition, and historical significance. This information becomes especially valuable as your collection grows and evolves.

Organizational Efficiency

Well-maintained records allow for efficient organization and easy retrieval of information. You can quickly locate specific coins, track changes in value, and identify any gaps or duplicates in your collection.

Insurance and Appraisal Purposes

Accurate documentation is essential for ensuring your coin collection and obtaining appropriate coverage. Additionally, well-documented records provide a valuable resource for appraisers when assessing the value of your collection.

Historical Significance

Your collection and the information you document contribute to the overall historical record of numismatics. By preserving the history of your coins, you contribute to the collective knowledge and understanding of the numismatic community.

Future Reference

Documentation serves as a valuable resource for future reference and research. It allows you to revisit your collection, share information with other collectors, and trace the provenance of your coins.

By recognizing the importance of record-keeping, you lay the foundation for an organized and informative collection that will benefit you and future generations of collectors.

CREATING A COIN INVENTORY

Creating a coin inventory is an essential step in documenting your collection. An inventory serves as a comprehensive list of your coins and provides a snapshot of your collection at any given time.

Start with Basic Information

Begin by recording basic information about each coin, including its name or description, denomination, date, country of origin, mint mark, and any unique identifiers.

Organize by Categories

Categorize your coins by series, type, or other relevant criteria. This helps to maintain order and facilitates easier searching and retrieval of information.

Utilize Spreadsheets or Digital Tools

Use spreadsheets or dedicated coin inventory software to create your inventory. These tools allow for easy updating, sorting, and filtering of information.

Include Additional Details

Expand your inventory by including additional details such as the coin's grade, condition, weight, diameter, composition, and any notable characteristics.

Assign Unique Identifiers

Assign unique identifiers, such as inventory numbers or personal identifiers, to each coin in your inventory. These identifiers facilitate quick identification and reference.

Include Acquisition Details

Document how and when each coin was acquired, including purchase dates, sources, and prices. This information helps establish provenance and enhances the historical significance of your collection.

Creating a comprehensive coin inventory provides a solid foundation for documenting and organizing your collection. It allows for easier management, identification, and retrieval of information.

CATALOGING AND DESCRIBING COINS

Cataloging and describing your coins in detail is crucial for providing a comprehensive overview of your collection. Consider the following aspects when cataloging and describing coins:

Detailed Descriptions

Provide detailed descriptions of each coin, including obverse and reverse designs, inscriptions, symbols, and notable features. Mention any errors or varieties that make the coin unique.

Grading and Condition

Assess the condition of each coin and assign a grade based on the established grading scale. Describe any wear, toning, or other characteristics that affect the coin's appearance or value.

Photographs

Supplement your descriptions with high-quality photographs of each coin. Capture both the obverse and reverse sides, ensuring clear and well-lit images that showcase the coin's details.

Provenance and History

Document the provenance and history of each coin, if known. Include information about previous owners, notable collections, or significant events associated with the coin.

Certifications and Appraisals

Note any certifications or appraisals received for specific coins. Include details such as the grading service, certification numbers, and appraisal values.

Cross-Referencing

Cross-reference your coin descriptions with the corresponding inventory numbers or unique identifiers assigned to each coin. This ensures an accurate linkage between your inventory and detailed descriptions.

By cataloging and describing your coins in detail, you create a comprehensive reference guide that captures the nuances and unique characteristics of each coin in your collection.

RESEARCHING AND DOCUMENTING THE HISTORY OF YOUR COINS

Researching and documenting the history of your coins adds depth and context to your collection. It allows you to uncover fascinating stories, historical connections, and the cultural significance of each coin. Consider the following steps when researching and documenting the history of your coins:

Numismatic Literature

Consult numismatic literature, books, and online resources specific to the coins in your collection. These sources provide valuable historical context, mintage figures, and information about notable varieties or minting errors.

Online Databases and Archives

Utilize online databases and archives dedicated to numismatics. These platforms offer access to historical documents, auction records, and detailed information about specific coins or series.

Numismatic Experts and Organizations

Seek the expertise of numismatic experts or consult with organizations specializing in specific coin series or historical periods. They can provide insights, answer questions, and help validate the historical information related to your coins.

Historical Research

Conduct broader historical research to understand the socio-political, economic, and cultural context in which your coins were minted. Explore the events, personalities, and historical milestones associated with the time period of your coins.

Documenting Findings

Record your research findings alongside the relevant coins in your collection. Include information about the coin's historical significance, the ruler or authority at the time of minting, and any notable historical events associated with the coin.

By researching and documenting the history of your coins, you gain a deeper appreciation for their significance and enrich the narrative of your collection. This information becomes a valuable resource for sharing stories, engaging with other collectors, and preserving the historical legacy of your coins.

CHAPTER 21

EXPLORING WORLD COIN SERIES:
FOCUS ON DIFFERENT COUNTRIES AND REGIONS

W orld coins offer a diverse range of designs, historical significance, and cultural exploration. In this chapter, we will delve into popular coin series from around the world, discuss collecting coins by country or region, and highlight the cultural and historical significance of world coins. By venturing beyond national borders, you can expand your collecting horizons and gain a deeper appreciation for the rich heritage and global impact of numismatics.

POPULAR COIN SERIES FROM AROUND THE WORLD

The world is filled with fascinating coin series that captivate collectors with their unique designs and historical context. Let's explore some popular coin series from different regions.

European Coin Series

The Eurozone countries offer an extensive range of coin series, such as the Euro commemorative coins, which celebrate important events, cultural icons, and historical milestones.

American Coin Series

The United States Mint produces a variety of coin series, including the America the Beautiful Quarters, Presidential Dollars, and commemorative coins that pay tribute to significant figures, landmarks, and historical events.

Asian Coin Series

Countries like China, Japan, and India have rich numismatic traditions. The Chinese Panda series, Japanese Yen coins, and Indian Rupee coins showcase the diverse cultural heritage and artistic excellence of these nations.

African Coin Series

African countries often feature unique coin series that highlight their natural resources, wildlife, and cultural traditions. The South African Krugerrand, Moroccan dirhams, and Namibian dollar coins are notable examples.

Oceanian Coin Series

The Pacific island nations, such as Australia and New Zealand, produce stunning coin series featuring indigenous flora and fauna, iconic landmarks, and cultural symbols. The Australian Kangaroo and Koala series and New Zealand Kiwi coins are highly sought after.

Latin American Coin Series

Latin American countries offer a rich assortment of coin series that reflect their history, culture, and famous figures. The Mexican Libertad, Argentine Peso, and Brazilian Real coins are among the notable examples.

These popular coin series provide collectors with an opportunity to explore different regions, immerse themselves in diverse cultures, and appreciate the unique designs and historical narratives represented on the coins.

COLLECTING COINS BY COUNTRY OR REGION

Collecting coins by country or region is a popular approach for many numismatists. Focusing on specific countries or regions allows collectors to delve deeper into the history, culture, and numismatic heritage of a particular area. Consider the following aspects when collecting coins by country or region:

Research and Study

Research the history, numismatic traditions, and notable coin series of the country or region you wish to collect. Study numismatic literature, online resources, and consult with experts to enhance your knowledge.

Set Collecting Goals

Define your collecting goals, whether it's acquiring a comprehensive set of coins from a particular country or region, focusing on specific historical periods, or collecting coins featuring specific themes or designs.

Acquiring Coins

Determine your acquisition strategy based on your collecting goals and budget. Explore coin dealers, online platforms, auctions, and coin shows to find the coins you desire. Consider joining numismatic clubs or forums that specialize in the country or region you are interested in to access a network of fellow collectors.

Quality and Condition

Pay attention to the quality and condition of the coins you acquire. Aim for coins in the best possible condition within your budget, as this can significantly impact their value and desirability.

Expand Your Knowledge

Continuously expand your knowledge about the country or region you are collecting. Explore the historical context of the coins, learn about the key figures, events, and cultural symbolism depicted on them, and understand the evolution of coin designs over time.

Collecting coins by country or region allows you to develop a deeper understanding of the cultural, historical, and artistic aspects associated with a specific geographic area. It enables you to build a focused collection that reflects your passion and interests.

UNDERSTANDING THE CULTURAL AND HISTORICAL SIGNIFICANCE OF WORLD COINS

World coins offer a window into the cultural and historical tapestry of different nations and regions. Understanding their significance enriches the collecting experience and provides a broader perspective on global history. Consider the following points to enhance your understanding of the cultural and historical significance of world coins:

Historical Context

Study the historical context in which coins were minted. Explore the significant events, rulers, and socio-economic factors that influenced the coinage of a particular country or region. Understanding the historical backdrop allows for a deeper appreciation of the coins' significance.

Cultural Symbolism

Coins often incorporate cultural symbols, icons, or figures that represent the identity and heritage of a nation. Research the symbolism behind these designs, such as national emblems, historical landmarks, or traditional motifs, to grasp their cultural significance.

Artistic Expression

World coins showcase a diverse range of artistic styles and techniques. Appreciate the artistic expression on the coins, including engravings, portraits, and intricate designs that reflect the prevailing artistic trends of their time.

National Identity

Coins serve as a tangible representation of a country's identity and sovereignty. Explore how coins have been used to assert national pride, commemorate historical events, or promote cultural heritage.

Historical Figures

Coins often feature portraits of significant historical figures, such as monarchs, political leaders, or cultural icons. Research these individuals to understand their impact and contributions to their respective countries.

By deepening your understanding of the cultural and historical significance of world coins, you gain a greater appreciation for their intrinsic value beyond their monetary worth. You develop a richer perspective on global history, culture, and the interconnectedness of different nations.

CHAPTER 22

COIN COLLECTING FOR KIDS:
ENGAGING YOUNG NUMISMATISTS IN THE HOBBY

C oin collecting is not only a hobby but also an educational and rewarding experience for children. In this chapter, we will explore the importance of coin collecting for children, provide fun and educational activities for young collectors, and offer tips for encouraging kids' interest in coins. By engaging children in this hobby, we can foster their curiosity, develop their learning skills, and cultivate a lifelong appreciation for numismatics.

INTRODUCTION TO COIN COLLECTING FOR CHILDREN

Introducing children to coin collecting at an early age can have numerous benefits. It promotes their intellectual development, hone their observation skills, encourages historical and cultural exploration, and instills a sense of responsibility and patience. Consider the following points when introducing coin collecting to children:

Start with Basic Concepts

Begin by explaining the basic concepts of coin collecting, such as the different denominations, coin designs, and the historical significance of coins. Use age-appropriate language and engaging visuals to capture their interest.

Teach about Coin Values

Introduce children to the concept of coin values and how they can vary based on factors like rarity, condition, and historical significance. Help them understand the difference between face value and collector value.

Emphasize History and Culture

Discuss the historical and cultural aspects associated with coins. Share stories about the origins of coins, the symbols and figures depicted on them, and the countries they represent. Highlight the stories behind special edition coins or commemorative coins.

Promote Observational Skills

Encourage children to observe and appreciate the details on coins. Help them identify the inscriptions, designs, and other distinguishing features. This promotes attention to detail and enhances their observation skills.

Provide Hands-On Experience

Allow children to handle and examine coins under supervision. Teach them how to hold coins properly and explain the importance of proper handling to avoid damage or contamination.

By introducing children to the world of coin collecting, we can spark their curiosity and lay the foundation for a lifelong passion for numismatics.

FUN AND EDUCATIONAL ACTIVITIES FOR YOUNG COLLECTORS

Engaging children in fun and educational activities related to coin collecting enhances their learning experience and makes the hobby enjoyable. Consider the following activities to involve young collectors in the world of coins:

Coin Hunts

Organize coin hunts where children can search for specific coins or series in a controlled environment. Hide coins around the house or garden and provide clues or maps to guide them. This activity promotes observation skills and excitement for finding new coins.

Coin Sorting and Organizing

Help children sort and organize their coins based on different criteria such as denomination, country, or theme. Provide trays or coin albums to keep their collections organized and easily accessible.

Coin Rubbings

Encourage children to create coin rubbings using plain paper and crayons. Place a coin under the paper and gently rub the crayon over it to reveal the coin's design. This activity allows them to appreciate the intricate details of coins.

Coin Designing

Let children explore their creativity by designing their own coins on paper or using online design tools. Encourage them to think about symbols, figures, or themes they would like to represent on their coins.

Coin Trivia and Quiz Games

Create trivia questions or quiz games about coins and numismatic history. Test children's knowledge and reward them for correct answers. This activity promotes learning and friendly competition.

Virtual Museum Tours

Take children on virtual museum tours that feature numismatic exhibits. Explore online collections and exhibitions to expose them to different types of coins, historical periods, and cultural contexts.

These fun and educational activities make coin collecting interactive and enjoyable for children, fostering their curiosity and expanding their knowledge.

TIPS FOR ENCOURAGING KIDS' INTEREST IN COINS

To sustain children's interest in coin collecting, it is important to provide ongoing support and encouragement. Consider the following tips to nurture kids' interest in coins:

Lead by Example

Actively participate in coin collecting alongside your child. Show enthusiasm for your own collection and share interesting stories about the coins you collect. This demonstrates your passion and encourages children to get involved.

Create a Coin collecting Space

Dedicate a designated space for your child's coin collecting activities. Set up a small table or desk with storage for coins, magnifying glasses, reference books, and other necessary supplies. This creates a dedicated space for exploration and learning.

Attend Coin Shows or Club Meetings

Take children to coin shows, local club meetings, or numismatic events. Exposing them to the wider numismatic community allows them to interact with experienced collectors, view diverse coin collections, and foster connections with other young collectors.

Incorporate Coins into Learning

Integrate coins into children's learning activities. For example, use coins to teach math concepts like addition, subtraction, or counting money. Incorporate historical lessons by discussing the coins used during specific historical periods.

Gift Coins and Starter Sets

Present children with special coins or starter sets as gifts for birthdays, holidays, or milestones. These gifts add to their collection and create a sense of excitement and ownership.

Support Research and Exploration

Encourage children to research and explore different aspects of coin collecting. Provide access to age-appropriate books, online resources, and numismatic websites. Encourage them to ask questions, seek answers, and share their findings.

By providing ongoing support, incorporating coins into learning experiences, and fostering a positive environment, you can cultivate and sustain children's interest in coin collecting.

CONCLUSION

Throughout the Chapters of *Coin Collecting for Beginners 2024*, I have had the privilege of sharing my knowledge and passion for the art of coin collecting. As a seasoned collector and dedicated numismatist, it has been my goal to provide a comprehensive guide that simplifies complex concepts, offers practical guidance, and inspires readers to embark on their own coin collecting journeys.

Coin collecting is a hobby that transcends mere acquisition and monetary value. It is an exploration of history, art, culture, and personal connection. The chapters of this book have covered a wide range of topics, from understanding the basics of coin collecting to exploring rare and valuable coins, from navigating the market to preserving and protecting one's collection. Each chapter has been carefully crafted to provide valuable insights and actionable information for beginners and enthusiasts alike.

In the early chapters, we laid the foundation by introducing the history and significance of numismatics, as well as the different types of coins and how to start a collection. We discussed the factors that determine the value of coins and identified coins with investment potential. With practical advice on goal setting, budgeting, and knowledge building, readers were prepared to embark on their coin collecting journeys.

As the book progressed, we delved into various aspects of the hobby, including collecting methods and approaches, the joys and benefits of coin collecting, and where to locate coins. Essential tools, preservation techniques, and grading methods were also covered to ensure that collectors had the necessary resources to maintain the longevity and integrity of their collections.

We explored specialized areas of numismatics, such as commemorative and special edition coins, bullion coins, and world coin series, allowing collectors to expand their horizons and appreciate the diversity and cultural significance of coins from different countries and regions.

Moreover, we recognized the importance of engaging young numismatists in the hobby, providing activities and tips to nurture their interest and cultivate a lifelong passion for coin collecting. By involving children in this enriching pursuit, we ensure the preservation and continuation of numismatic knowledge for generations to come.

As I reflect on the journey we have taken together in this book, I am filled with a sense of gratitude and fulfillment. It has been my sincerest hope to share my knowledge and passion for coin collecting in a way that resonates with readers, encouraging them to embrace this fascinating hobby and embark on their own collecting adventures.

I urge you to continue exploring, learning, and sharing your love for coins. Embrace the thrill of the hunt, the joy of discovery, and the connections that coins forge with history and culture. Let the chapters of this book serve as a guide, a companion, and a source of inspiration as you delve deeper into the captivating world of numismatics.

Remember, coin collecting is a lifelong pursuit that offers endless opportunities for growth, learning, and enjoyment. Whether you are a beginner or an experienced collector, may this book be a valuable resource that empowers you to navigate the intricate realm of coin collecting with confidence and enthusiasm.

Thank you for joining me on this numismatic journey, and may your future coin collecting endeavors be filled with excitement, knowledge, and the fulfillment that comes from preserving history in the palm of your hand.